CW00661212

The MONOCLE
Travel Guide Series

31 (M)

Melbourne

All rights reserved. No part of this
publication may be reproduced or
transmitted in any form or by any
means, electronic or mechanical,
including photocopy or any
storage and retrieval system,
without permission in writing
from the publisher.

Respect copyrights,
encourage creativity!

For more information,
please visit *gestalten.com*

Bibliographic information
published by the Deutsche
Nationalbibliothek: The Deutsche
Nationalbibliothek lists this
publication in the Deutsche
Nationalbibliografie; detailed
bibliographic data are available
online at *dnb.d-nb.de*

This book was printed on
paper certified by the FSC®

Monocle editor in chief
and chairman: *Tyler Brûlé*
Monocle editor: *Andrew Tuck*
Books editor: *Joe Pickard*
Guide editor: *Mikaela Aitken*

Designed by *Monocle*
Proofreading by *Monocle*
Typeset in *Plantin & Helvetica*

Printed by *Offsetdruckerei
Grammlich, Pliezhausen*

Made in Germany

Published by *Gestalten*, Berlin 2018
ISBN 978-3-89955-951-4

© Die Gestalten Verlag GmbH &
Co. KG, Berlin 2018

Welcome
—— Beside the bayside

Modern Melbourne is a *sprawling metropolis* that's growing faster than it has at any other point in its two-century-long history. Teetering around five million, the population is set to double by 2050, a fact that has local government scurrying to improve transport networks and think about sustainable housing solutions.

Thankfully, work has begun on an AU$11bn underground metro tunnel (due for completion in 2025), heavy investments have been made into developing affordable homes and world-first regulations are in place to help protect small-business owners and late-night licensees.

This *forward-thinking* approach characterises the city's commitment to its superlative cultural outposts, pristine parks and *diverse population*. But perhaps what's most unique is Melbourne's knack of layering its offering. Makers and indie bookshops shimmy up to live-music venues and cutting-edge galleries nestle neatly into residential neighbourhoods. And that's before you mention the abundance of mouth-watering brunch, lunch and dinner menus, faultless all-Australian wine lists and *welcoming hospitality* found across the city.

While this outward-facing state capital expands in leaps and bounds, the resident *Melburnians* hold fast to their laidback lifestyle. It's little wonder that creative talent and *entrepreneurs* drop anchor here and, after your visit, we think you might be tempted to do the same. Turn the page to find out what all the fuss is about. — (M)

Contents
— Navigating the city

Use the key below to help navigate the guide section by section.

H Hotels

F Food and drink

R Retail

T Things we'd buy

E Essays

C Culture

D Design and architecture

S Sport and fitness

W Walks

Map
—— Find a way

In terms of sheer geographical span, Melbourne is one of the 10 largest cities in the world. Naturally then, it has a diverse crop of neighbourhoods to choose from. Fitzroy, Brunswick, Collingwood and Thornbury in the inner-north are magnets for the city's hipster crowd. Begin with Smith, Gertrude, Lygon and Brunswick streets for phenomenally good cafés and locally made wares.

In the west, former working-class suburbs Footscray, Yarraville and Seddon are experiencing a renaissance, while in the east the affluent areas of Kew and Hawthorn are characterised by large, detached homes and a growing cohort of charming cafés. South of the Yarra River is a cluster of cultural institutions, followed by the rapidly regenerating suburb of South Melbourne.

On the bay sits St Kilda, with its art deco landmarks and beach (of sorts). Then there's the CBD, where skyscrapers flank warrens of laneways. This is where you'll find some of the best tables, biggest retailers and newest galleries.

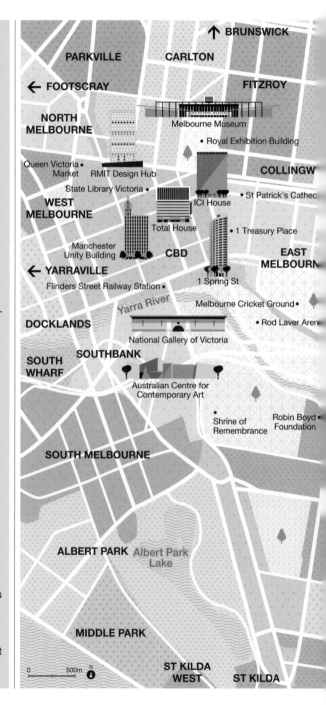

↑ BRUNSWICK

PARKVILLE   CARLTON

← FOOTSCRAY   FITZROY

NORTH MELBOURNE

Melbourne Museum

• Royal Exhibition Building

Queen Victoria Market   RMIT Design Hub

COLLINGW

State Library Victoria •

WEST MELBOURNE   ICI House   • St Patrick's Cathed

Total House   • 1 Treasury Place

Manchester Unity Building   CBD   EAST MELBOURN

← YARRAVILLE

1 Spring St

Flinders Street Railway Station •

Melbourne Cricket Ground •

Yarra River

DOCKLANDS   • Rod Laver Aren

National Gallery of Victoria

SOUTH WHARF   SOUTHBANK

Australian Centre for Contemporary Art

Shrine of Remembrance   Robin Boyd • Foundation

SOUTH MELBOURNE

ALBERT PARK   Albert Park Lake

MIDDLE PARK

0   500m   N

ST KILDA WEST   ST KILDA

Need to know
—— Get to grips with the basics

Secret locations
The fun is in the finding

In most cities, a venue that's tucked away down several twists and turns of a shady alley, or out of sight up neverending flights of stairs, may find it difficult to attract footfall. Not so in Melbourne. The harder the place is to find or the more obscure the previous tenants, the better: Melburnians favour the elusive. So when in town, do as they do and hunt out hidden haunts such as The Croft Institute, Section 8, Ferdydurke, Switchboard Café and Northside Boulders' Brunswick climbing centre.

Nightlife
The show must go on

A recent spate of late-night, alcohol-fuelled incidents in Australia has led Sydney and Brisbane to clamp down on bars and clubs. Melbourne has opted for a different tack and introduced evening activities that aren't centred around getting trollied (although boozy beverages are, of course, still available), including outdoor cinema screenings, food markets and cultural festivals.

Addresses
Numbers game

Melbourne's CBD follows a standard grid format. So you would think navigation would be a breeze, right? Wrong. Streets outside of these ordered city blocks stretch on, passing through several neighbourhoods and, upon entering a new suburb, the numbers reset. Within the same pocket of town there may be three iterations of 33 Albion Street. Note down the postcode if you want to end up at the right destination.

To further muddle things, prominent neighbourhood names also appear as street names – but on the other side of town. Fitzroy Street in St Kilda and Brunswick Street in Fitzroy are two confusing cases in point.

Café culture
Bean there, done that

While the dispute rages on over whether it was Sydney or Wellington that first served that legendary Antipodean brew known as the flat white, Melbourne forges ahead with its world-renowned coffee culture. Prepare to consume coffee in all its forms, multiple times a day. There are some 5,000 cafés, also offering unbeatable brunches, sharp design and friendly service.

Working in a café in Melbourne is a coveted career choice. In fact, these well-paid positions attract talented and enthusiastic staff who are either highly trained baristas or freelancers and students taking a break from their daily grind.

Out of town
Breath of fresh air

Sandwiched between the coast and the countryside, Victoria's capital is an ideal launchpad for touring the rest of the state. Spend a day or two exploring the varied terroirs and the wines that result, hop between the beaches along the Great Ocean Road, hike through the Grampians or catch a taste of country life in towns such as Daylesford, Bendigo and Castlemaine.

Australian Rules football
The only game in town

According to Melburnians, there is only one game: Australian Rules football. It was born in Melbourne, with the organised league (AFL) officially kicking off in 1897. Of the 18 clubs currently playing in the men's competition, nine are based in the city.

Between March and September the men's games consume pubs and sporting fields until the explosive Grand Final hits Melbourne in late September. The women's league takes place during February and March.

I told you, we may have huge hands but we're playing 'footy'

Tram is the only way to travel!

Trams
Still on track

The first tram in Melbourne trundled along the tracks in 1885 and by 1916 the network was carrying more than 100 million passengers a year.

This is the only Australian city to maintain this mode of public transport. There's a Free Tram Zone in the CBD and Docklands and if you take the City Circle loop there's a chance you'll be on board the classic W-class models, built between 1923 and 1956.

Money matters
Tipping and splitting

Hospitality wages are excellent here so no one will be offended if you don't tip. However, if the service is outstanding (and more often than not it is) it's polite to round up the bill or add 10 to 15 per cent. An automatic 10 per cent may also be added if it's a public holiday.

It's also worth noting that restaurants and cafés don't always appreciate divvying up bills – in fact, some places will flat out refuse. Best to have one person put it on plastic, and sort it out between yourselves later, or have the correct cash at the ready.

Urban renewal
New lease of life

During the 1980s, Melbourne's CBD fell victim to the "doughnut effect". Come evenings and weekends, it was a ghost town, devoid of residents or visitors and with shops and restaurants closed.

A central city-planning review led by city council and state government in the late 1990s sought to rectify this. Changes included more relaxed alcohol-licensing laws, protection for live-music and late-night venues and subsidising studio rent for artists. Now the laneways are full of restaurants, shops and galleries that open in the evenings and weekends, plus there's a spike in residency – a case study in successful urban revival.

Weather
Never a dull moment

Melbourne's weather can be notoriously fickle. Even when the morning report predicts a sun-filled day, a thunderstorm can roll in, wreak havoc and roll out within the space of half an hour. And counter to the stereotypes of Australia as a hot, sun-scorched country, winters in Melbourne can be chilly affairs, with temperatures occasionally dropping to freezing. Having said that, heat waves in January are also common.

The trick? Pack layers that both combat cold snaps and protect you from the searing sun, as well as an umbrella to keep yourself dry – after all, the weather gamble is all part of the fun.

Our top picks:

01 **The Kettle Black:** Start your day with some tasty tucker. *see page 30*

02 **Heide Museum of Modern Art:** A roster of talent in modernist digs. *see page 91*

03 **Seven Seeds:** Melbourne coffee at its very best. *see page 26*

04 **Supernormal:** One of the city's best food joints. *see page 32*

05 **National Gallery of Victoria:** An important museum in an equally impressive building. *see page 96*

06 **Readings Books:** Pick up some local literature. *see page 67*

07 **Total House:** This brutalist office block looks like a floating television. *see page 114*

08 **City Wine Shop:** Drink in the state's formidable wine offering. *see page 49*

09 **Mr Kitly:** Australian and Japanese ceramics, tableware and more. *see page 51*

10 **Brighton Baths Health Club:** Take a dip in Port Phillip Bay. *see page 126*

Looks like it'll snow later!

Hotels
—— Make yourself at home

For a city packed to the rafters with restaurateurs, entrepreneurs and designers, it's perplexing that Melbourne's hotel scene isn't a little more progressive. The talent is most definitely present but it seems the food and retail industries are the sexier options for business owners. Which means when it comes to finding the best place to rest your head in Melbourne, there's a woeful lack of clever independent or design-led offerings.

But don't fret – we've found locations that fly the flag for both beloved institutions and staunch chains. We've also gone off-piste and zipped across the state to find our three favourite out-of-town options. Looking ahead, we hope the prospect of the owner of Jackalope opening a city location in 2020 will spur a new generation of Melbourne hoteliers.

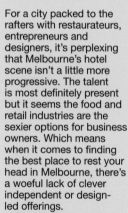

② QT Melbourne, CBD
Industrial evolution

Event Hotels & Resorts opened this central Melbourne location in 2016, the group's first foray into Victoria's capital. The staff – outfitted in house uniforms and wigs – are the epitome of Australia's renowned sunny service, and the public interiors by Nic Graham recall Melbourne's jaunty laneways.

The 188 rooms have a contemporary industrial feel, with concrete and timber surfaces that are offset by specially commissioned rugs and contemporary art. For the best outlook, request a room facing Russell Street.
133 Russell Street, 3000
+61 (0)3 8636 8800
qthotelsandresorts.com

MONOCLE COMMENT: Bistro and cocktail stop-off Pascale Bar & Grill, sleek sundowner bar Rooftop, Asian fusion restaurant Hot Sauce and Japanese knife shop Tanto all bolster the on-site offering.

❶ The Prince, St Kilda
On the waterfront

Visitors to Melbourne looking for picture-postcard ocean views are likely to be a little disappointed but The Prince in St Kilda offers the next best thing. The hotel's streamlined art deco balconies give the heritage-listed 1937 building the air of a lofty ocean liner, while granting guests views of the palm trees lining the waterfront.

The current 39-room venue opened in 1999 but there has been a guesthouse on this site since the 1860s so The Prince is no stranger to hospitality. A tasteful refurbishment in 2017 saw a subtle beachside theme rolled out across the building in a palette of earthy pastels. All rooms are kitted out with Kevin Murphy hair products and Bose speakers.
2 Acland Street, 3182
+61 (0)3 9536 1111
theprince.com.au

MONOCLE COMMENT: The on-site Prince Bandroom is a headliner in its own right, having hosted an international line-up of acts including Lenny Kravitz, Pink and Goldfrapp.

❸

Park Hyatt Melbourne,
East Melbourne
Quiet achiever

Located behind the Old
Treasury Building, surrounded
by century-old elms, the Park
Hyatt Melbourne feels tranquil
while still being a stone's throw
from the CBD. It also benefits
from the five-star grandeur that
comes with operating under
the umbrella of a well-run
international chain.

A flashy lobby (think lots
of marble, mahogany and
gold) connects the two towers
housing 240 comfortable
rooms, 24 of which are suites.
For city views, we recommend
requesting a stay in the Park
Tower. In 2018 a refresh of
the rooms was completed by
British textile designer and
artist David Parsons.

1 Parliament Square, 3002
+61 (0)3 9224 1234
melbourne.park.hyatt.com

MONOCLE COMMENT:
A stalwart option for great
service and five-star luxury.

4

Ovolo Laneways, CBD
Simple pleasures

This 43-room hotel was Hong Kong hotelier Ovolo's first Australian outpost. With two impressive Sydney addresses opening since, this Melbourne iteration now feels a little tired. But in a city craving inventive and dependable hotel options, it's still a solid choice.

The reception area is brief, rooms tidy and functional, and breakfast a simple grab-and-go affair. Its location is ideal for exploring Chinatown and the CBD's laneway haunts.
19 Little Bourke Street, 3000
+61 (0)3 8692 0777
ovolohotels.com.au

MONOCLE COMMENT: The three penthouse suites are great for larger groups, with a fridge full of beers and a rooftop terrace for hosting.

5

InterContinental Melbourne The Rialto, CBD
History repeated

The neo-gothic half of InterContinental's Melbourne address dates back to the gold rush days of the 1890s. The series of apartments, offices and wool and wheat stores may have been forgotten by the 1960s but, after careful restoration of the original building and construction of a second structure to mirror it, a hotel moved in during the 1980s and InterContinental took ownership in 2008.

Today this 253-room hotel is a sound choice for business travellers, with a business centre and 13 meeting rooms, four eating and drinking outposts, 24-hour room service, a rooftop pool and gym, plus a day spa. The rooms are simple, with subdued furnishings, plush linens and cream marble counters in the bathrooms.
495 Collins Street, 3000
+61 (0)3 8627 1400
melbourne.intercontinental.com

MONOCLE COMMENT: The glass atrium between the two buildings adds a lofty appeal. Pull up a seat at one of the bars to take in the architecture.

⑥

Microluxe, various locations
Feel like you belong

British architect Ben Edwards is the brains behind this refreshing approach to guesthouses. "When you stay somewhere, you want to feel like a local," he says of his small stays in buzzy Melbourne neighbourhoods. The first (*pictured*) opened in 2016 in Fitzroy, between the major cultural and dining strips of Brunswick and Smith streets. Naturally, Studio Edwards designed the interiors but each site also features quality makers such as Loom Towels (linens), Ben-Tovim (furniture and light fittings) and Leif (soap and shampoo). *micro-luxe.com*

MONOCLE COMMENT: Watch this space: Edwards is on the hunt for properties beyond his current Fitzroy and North Fitzroy portfolio.

⑦

The Hotel Windsor, CBD
A grand affair

This Victorian structure was built in 1883 during the world's love affair with grand hotels. In fact, the Hotel Windsor is a predecessor to hotels such as as Raffles in Singapore, The Savoy in London and The Plaza in New York.

Finding a balance between respecting its history and updating became a sore topic between passionate locals and Halim Group, its owners since 2008. But while it's set to undergo a AU$330m redevelopment between 2018 and 2020 (adding almost 300 rooms and eight bars and restaurants), the original glamour of its baroque-style ballroom, heritage suites, sweeping staircase and broad hallways (built wide to accommodate women's hoop dresses) will remain. *111 Spring Street, 3000*
+61 (0)3 9633 6000
thehotelwindsor.com.au

MONOCLE COMMENT: The federal constitution was fine-tuned here and the Cricketers Bar is where the British cricket team unwinds post match.

8

The Olsen, South Yarra
Art of the city

Part of the Art Series – which
has seven outposts across
the country, each dedicated
to the work of a different
contemporary Australian
artist – this 224-room, glass-
encased tower in South Yarra
evokes the spirited paintings
of Dr John Olsen. On top of
uninterrupted views of the
city, the hotel offers guests
hire of its bikes, scooters and
smart cars to help explore the
surrounding area.

The art theme runs
throughout with Olsen prints
and stacks of glossy art books
in every room. There's even an
in-house art curator.
637-641 Chapel Street, 3141
+61 (0)3 9040 1222
artserieshotels.com.au

MONOCLE COMMENT: When
exiting the hotel along Chapel
Street, glance up for a worm's-
eye view of the glass-bottomed,
overhanging swimming pool.

Well, isn't this lovely?

9

Coppersmith Hotel,
South Melbourne
Boutique bolthole

A mere toss of a ball from
Albert Park and its sporting
facilities, this 15-room hotel
opened in its current guise
in 2014 after operating as the
Cricket Club Hotel since the
1870s. Courtesy of design firm
Hassell, rooms are decked
out in a tasteful monochrome
palette and come with custom
lighting by Ross Gardam and
stools from Jardan (*see page
54*). The rooftop features a
timber-decked terrace that
offers fine views over the south
Melbourne skyline, while the
ground floor is occupied by
a heaving bar and bistro.
435 Clarendon Street, 3205
+61 (0)3 8696 7777
coppersmithhotel.com.au

MONOCLE COMMENT: The
hotel's name pays homage to
South Melbourne coppersmith
Ebenezer Drummond Menzies
Thompson, a lifelong resident
of the suburb and its mayor
from 1913 to 1914.

Pieds-à-terre
—

For hotel alternatives, try
stylist Lynda Gardener's Fitzroy
North apartment The White
Room. Alternatively, concept
retailer The Standard Store
has a double-bedder above
its Fitzroy shop.
*thewhitehousedaylesford.com.
au; thestandardstore.com.au*

Out of town
Get away from it all

1

Brae, Birregurra
Taste of the country

Visiting one of the state's most
famed dining spots is not
the only reason to make the
90-minute drive southwest
of the city to this estate. It also
houses six suites, which reflect
owner and chef Dan Hunter's
approach to both design
and food.

Throughout, exposed red-
brick and timber interiors are
paired with slate floors and
brass fittings. Each suite has
a turntable and cocktail bar,
as well as panoramic views of
the countryside, all of which
can be enjoyed from the tub.
4285 Cape Otway Road, 3242
+61 (0)3 5236 2226
braerestaurant.com

MONOCLE COMMENT: Brae's
accolades include being ranked
44th in the 2017 list of the
world's 50 best restaurants.

2

Jackalope, Mornington
Peninsula
Story to tell

This 45-room vineyard
getaway, nestled among the
gum trees of the Mornington
Peninsula, is the first hotel
from entrepreneur Louis Li.
Guests are greeted by local
artist Emily Floyd's seven-
metre-tall sculpture of the
eponymous jackalope,
a mythical creature which is
half jack rabbit, half antelope.

"Not a lot of high-end hotels
have a strong site narrative these
days," says Li, and Jackalope
certainly breaks the mould.
A subtle alchemy theme runs
throughout the hotel: enigmatic
symbols line the corridors and
a tasteful colour palette of black
and gold prevails.

Suites boast king-size beds
by AH Beard (Australia's oldest
mattress-maker) and feature
charred-timber walls that riff
on the texture of wine barrels.
166 Balnarring Road, 3926
+61 (0)3 5931 2500
jackalopehotels.com

MONOCLE COMMENT:
The black-tiled, 30-metre
infinity pool overlooks the
mesmerising stripes of the
vineyard. Hop in.

3

The Farmhouse at Meletos,
Yarra Valley
Growing appeal

This Tuscan-inspired, 23-room guesthouse in Yarra Valley – a region that has long lured people out of the city – overlooks 80 hectares of vineyards, crab-apple orchards and manicured vegetable plots. Spread across a series of century-old farm buildings, each cosy room has an ensuite. The on-site regional café, restaurant and deli are stocked with fresh ingredients from the grounds and offer vistas stretching over the Great Dividing Range.
*12 Saint Huberts Road,
Coldstream, 3770
+61 (0)3 8727 3030
meletos.com*

MONOCLE COMMENT: Hatha and Vinyasa classes take place on the lawn before breakfast.

Don't mind me, just testing!

Food and drink
—— Melbourne on a plate

The unmistakable energy of Melbourne's food-and-drink scene makes it one of the world's most rewarding cities for culinary exploration. From strong coffee and buttery croissants through to the sharpest end of fine dining, there's an inspired creativity and attention to detail at play here, elevating even the simplest ideas to extraordinary new heights.

Perhaps more importantly though, this is a city that loves to eat out. For Melburnians, food is written about, photographed, discussed and debated just as voraciously as it's tasted.

Within this chapter you'll find an assortment of venues to suit any circumstance or mood. From stand-up espresso spots and buzzy brunch temples to tucked-away trattorias and low-lit neighbourhood wine bars, the food and drink offerings in Melbourne are neverending. We hope you're hungry.

Coffee shops
Espresso yourself

1
Auction Rooms,
North Melbourne
Successful bid

An early adopter of the city's speciality coffee wave, this impressively remodelled former auctioneers' quarters is serious about its beans. Founded by the team behind nearby Small Batch roastery, it's since been acquired by another of Melbourne's coffee super-groups and is a haven for coffee fans looking to try more than espresso.

Alongside filter coffee that uses single-origin beans from Guatemala, Kenya and Ethiopia, there are exemplary flat whites made with Small Batch's Candyman espresso blend and iced sparkling filter coffees come summer. The food is also excellent.
103-107 Errol Street, 3051
+61 (0)3 9326 7749
auctionroomscafe.com.au

❷
Vacation, CBD
Holiday spirit

The team behind this pint-sized, pastel-hued café have a history of creating venues that Melburnians go crazy for. Having settled on a winning formula, they've become masters of food, coffee, service and interiors.

Though small, the space is always relaxed, making it popular with corporate suits craving a break. The staff are approachable – you'll never be sneered at for ordering a cappuccino – and both house blends and single origins are available to take home. If the sun's out, look no further than the wonderfully refreshing pink grapefruit spritz: cold-brew coffee on ice topped with pink grapefruit soda.
1 Exhibition Street, 3000
+61 (0)3 9662 2013
itsavacation.com

3

Padre, Brunswick East
Easygoing affair

While other Brunswick cafés heave with freelancers and hungover brunch-goers, Padre maintains an air of effortless zen. With a mix of communal seating and tables for two, the light-filled space draws a down-to-earth crowd thanks to its great coffee and a handful of pastries and sweet treats.

Flat whites made from the excellent house-roasted espresso blend are popular and a great excuse to stay a while. You'll also find cold brew, filter coffee and rotating single origins to have in-house, plus a range of beans, merchandise and accoutrements to take home.
*438-440 Lygon Street, 3057
+61 (0)3 9381 1881
padrecoffee.com.au*

4

Seven Seeds, Carlton
Reap what you sow

Behind an unremarkable façade in backstreet Carlton lies the epicentre of Melbourne coffee. Launched in 2008 by Mark Dundon (considered the city's godfather of speciality coffee), Seeds has influenced a generation of wannabe roasters, baristas and café-owners – and spawned imitators aplenty.

Responsibly sourced beans are a given here, with Dundon and co making regular trips to obscure corners of the globe to connect with farmers. Weekly cupping (coffee-tasting) sessions are a good education and the café menu alone justifies a visit. Check out sister venues Traveller and Brother Baba Budan, both in the CBD.
*106-114 Berkeley Street, 3053
+61 (0)3 9347 8664
sevenseeds.com.au*

Espresso bars

01 Dukes Coffee Roasters, CBD: Sure, Melbourne does great brunch spots but sometimes leaning at a bar with an espresso and the day's papers is all you really need. Frequented by students and creatives alike, Dukes does outstanding house-roasted coffee and quality pastries with minimal fuss and maximum style.
dukescoffee.com.au

02 Patricia Coffee Brewers, CBD: Standing-room-only espresso makes perfect sense in the legal district, which is why this elegant little brew bar is rarely quiet. Owner Bowen Holden came through the Seven Seeds lineage (*opposite*) so he knows his beans – expect exemplary espresso, cold brew and filter, plus a tasty selection of pastries.
patriciacoffee.com.au

03 Everyday Coffee Midtown, CBD: Prohibitive mid-city rent doesn't always spell doom – sometimes it just generates a willingness to downsize. The younger sibling of Everyday Coffee in Collingwood, Midtown brews its own brand of coffee, which might include a filter roast from Ethiopia or a complex Rwandan espresso.
everyday-coffee.com

5
Market Lane Coffee, South Yarra
Brew it yourself

Founded in 2009 by coffee importer Fleur Studd and roaster Jason Scheltus, Market Lane is one of Melbourne's top coffee retailers. With six outlets across the city, the group's Prahran outpost is considered the flagship.

Studd is one of the country's foremost importers of quality green beans so provenance, seasonality and education are a big focus here. Staff are trained to share their wisdom and there are free tasting sessions each week. A superior range of beans suits any brewing method, plus there's both coffee-making equipment and books to peruse as you wait.
Shop 13, Prahran Market, 163 Commercial Road, 3141
+61 (0)3 9804 7434
marketlane.com.au

I take my coffee with pancakes

Brunch
Mid-morning munching

1
Smith Street Alimentari, Collingwood
Stick with the classics

With excellent produce-driven fare served in elegant, old-world surrounds, this husband-and-wife-run café and deli is a sanctuary on Smith Street. The all-day menu journeys through the Mediterranean and the Middle East, delivering breakfast classics along with delicious slow-roasted rotisserie meats and seasonal salads. A seat in the sunny courtyard with a glass of rosé in one hand and a good book in the other makes for a perfect Melbourne moment.
302-304 Smith Street, 3066
+61 (0)3 9416 1666
alimentari.com.au

2

Wide Open Road, Brunswick
Bean feast

Named after a song by seminal
1980s Australian alt-rock band
The Triffids, this backstreet
Brunswick brunch spot was
a pioneer of Melbourne's
now ubiquitous "renovated
industrial space turns coffee
roastery café" genre. Brunches
here may be rowdy but they're
never boring and there's a good
chance you'll brush shoulders
with unassuming local
musicians and artists as they
line up for their morning fix.

   Alongside the standard egg
offerings, the all-day brunch
menu lists classics such as
avocado with salsa and dukkah
on sourdough. Coffee here is
excellent (it's all roasted on
site) and comes in the form
of espresso, filter, pour-over,
cold drip and more.
274 Barkly Street, 3056
+61 (0)3 9010 9298
wideopenroad.com.au

4

Short Round, Thornbury
Waffle on

Thornbury's recent evolution
has seen the once-desolate high
street develop into a vibrant
café, bar and retail precinct
where you can happily spend
a day exploring. Run by sisters
Libby and Clare Cairns,
this lovely café occupies a
handsomely refurbished
former pet shop.

Brunch is served all day
and includes everything from
toasted waffles with berries,
lemon curd, fresh ricotta and
pistachios to classic avocado on
toast – served here with halloumi
and a poached egg. Along
with great coffee, there are
regional wines and brunch
cocktails such as the mint-
and-lemon iced tea laced
with Sailor Jerry spiced rum.
731 High Street, 3071
+61 (0)3 9484 3904.
shortround.com.au

Must-try
Smashed avocado from
Archie's All Day, Fitzroy
No visit to Melbourne is
complete without the requisite
"smashed avo" brunch and
this textural delight is an
excellent example. Toasted
sourdough comes crowned
with a generous jumble of
chunky avocado and regional
goat's feta enlivened with
parsley, mint, lemon, sumac
and dukkah.
archiesallday.com

3

Mina No Ie, Collingwood
Clean eating

The presiding ethos here is to
present "simple, life-affirming
dishes that provide energy,
health, comfort and balance" –
a concept that seems perfectly
achievable in the graceful,
uncomplicated zen of Mina
No Ie's airy, plant-filled
warehouse interior. This is
where Collingwood locals
come seeking atonement for
their weekend sins and the
organic Japanese menu does
much to aid the cause.

From the open kitchen
you'll see food being carefully
prepared, with homely dishes
such as "Mum's scrambled
eggs" (with spring onions,
tamari, salad and rice) or
miso-baked eggs (baked with
sweet miso, roasted aubergine,
butternut pumpkin and
provolone cheese served with
toast) providing a wholesome
alternative to the usual fry up.
33 Peel Street, 3066
+61 (0)3 9417 7749
minanoie.com

6

The Farm Café, Abbotsford
Bumper harvest

While there's an undeniable allure to Melbourne's laneways and inner-city streets, time spent in its more leafy open spaces always presents great reward. One such spot is the riverside parkland surrounding Abbotsford Convent, with its arts precinct, farmers' markets, children's farm and wonderful organic café by the Yarra.

The menu includes hits such as pan-fried brioche French toast with poached rhubarb, maple cream and pecan crumb, and healthy salads of leafy greens, quinoa, avocado and mixed seeds. Finish with a stroll along the Yarra Bend trail.
*Collingwood Children's Farm,
18 Saint Heliers Street, 3067
+61 (0)3 9415 6581
farmcafe.com.au*

5

The Kettle Black,
South Melbourne
Breakfast of champions

Housed in a stunningly restored Victorian terrace house a stone's throw from the Botanical Gardens, this popular haunt could easily win the title of Melbourne's most photogenic café. Sweet and savoury hankerings are given equal billing and satisfied in the most inventive ways by a technique-driven, hyper-seasonal menu.

Those with a sweet tooth should try the coconut chia pudding with citrus, blood-orange-and-raspberry sorbet and toasted coconut, while savoury fans will delight in the miso-cured salmon with barley salad, ginger dressing and poached egg. You'll also find a range of boozy breakfast cocktails (Wasabi Bloody Mary or Espresso Martini, anyone?) plus cold-pressed juice and excellent coffee.
*50 Albert Road, 3205
+61 (0)3 9088 0721
thekettleblack.com.au*

1

Cumulus Inc, CBD
Head in the clouds

Few venues manage to glide between breakfast, business lunch and romantic dinner as effortlessly and convincingly as this laneway original. In the morning, the elegant light-filled space makes a fine perch for catching up on the day's news with a flat white and a breakfast set (boiled egg, sourdough, preserves, yoghurt and juice).

Come nightfall, Andrew McConnell's produce-driven menu switches gear to inspired, share-friendly dining. Start with a glass of Tasmanian fizz and some native oysters then move on to the tuna tartare with crushed peas – just be sure to factor in the signature slow-roasted lamb shoulder.

The service is smart, the wine list diverse and the buzz undeniable. Nightcap? Take the stairs to sibling bar Cumulus Up, one floor above.
45 Flinders Lane, 3000
+61 (0)3 9650 1445
cumulusinc.com.au

7

Higher Ground, CBD
Peak performance

The team behind this CBD brunch spot is also responsible for excellent cafés, including The Kettle Black (*see opposite*) and Top Paddock. Here they've taken things to entirely new levels. With its soaring ceilings and multilevel seating, the heritage-listed former powerhouse feels less café and more elegant hotel lobby.

The seasonal menu allows for simplicity but you would be mad not to partake of the more inventive fare. Think poached eggs with white asparagus, Comté, tarragon and rye toast, or ricotta hotcakes scattered with berries, seeds and flowers. The coffee is top notch too.
650 Little Bourke Street, 3000
+61 (0)3 8899 6219
highergroundmelbourne.com.au

②

Supernormal, CBD
Bao wow

It can be tricky defining
Supernormal to a non-native.
While the menu may be
part Japanese, part Chinese
and part Korean, the serious
wine-slinging, come-anytime
approach is undeniably
Melbourne. Part of chef-
restaurateur Andrew
McConnell's stable, it's
"canteen" by extraction but
not execution. The minimal,
timber-clad space features a
long open kitchen and bar
(plenty of theatre if you're
dining solo) and is accented
with flashes of pink neon.

Start with a lobster roll and
the twice-cooked duck bao,
then move on to the whole
snapper with burnt butter and
kombu. Just leave room for the
peanut-butter parfait at the
sweet end. And if you get stuck,
ask the smart and helpful staff.
180 Flinders Lane, 3000
+61 (0)3 9650 8688
supernormal.net.au

3

Thanh Ha 2, Richmond
Freshen up

Every inner-city Melburnian has their favourite go-to in Richmond's Little Saigon and it's easy to see why this brightly lit Victoria Street diner is packed most nights. The family-run spot has TVs playing sports in the corner and serves authentic Vietnamese food that's flavoursome, fragrant and bursting with freshness.

Thanh Ha 2 is also a great place to try something new and the efficient staff will happily guide you through the more obscure regional specialities. The *goi ga* (chicken coleslaw) balances acidity, sweetness and a thrilling mix of textures while the *banh cuon* (steamed rice-paper rolls with prawn or pork) will have you coming back for more. It's "bring your own" too, so be sure to pick up a bottle of dry local riesling en route.
120 Victoria Street, 3121
+61 (0)3 9421 6219

4

Kaprica, Carlton
Slice of the action

The fact that this charmingly low-fi artisan pizzeria is located in a renovated garage on the outer edge of Carlton's Little Italy speaks volumes: you'll find few cultural – or culinary – parallels with the gingham-clad tourist traps a few streets away. *Pizzaiolo* and owner Pietro Barbagallo led the charge with authentic thin-crust pizza in Brunswick East almost two decades ago and he hasn't lost his touch.

Overlooking leafy Lincoln Square South, this homely space has a rustic authenticity reminiscent of the backstreets of Trastevere. The pizza is excellent, the wine list accessible and the atmosphere casual. Try the broccoli pizza with mozzarella, chilli and lemon.
19 Lincoln Square, 3053
+61 (0)3 9347 1138

5

Emilia, CBD
Pride of place

Hyper-regional Italian cuisine (Venetian, Sicilian, Sardinian) has taken hold in Melbourne in recent times as tastes have ventured beyond the carb-laden clichés of "Italian food". Run by a team of Modena expats, this trattoria is an homage to the salumi-studded fare of Emilia-Romagna, birthplace of balsamic vinegar and prosciutto di Parma.

The food – like the dining room – is equal parts rustic and refined. Lunch might be a glass of sangiovese and a quick plate of tortelloni with mortadella, parmesan and walnuts, while evenings bring a low-lit, romantic glow that will have you saying "*perché no*" ("why not") to that second bottle.
Gills Alley, 3000
+61 (0)3 9670 7214
emiliamelbourne.com.au

City staples

01 France Soir, South Yarra: This timeless neighbourhood bistro has been serving steak frites and aged French red to well-heeled South Yarra residents since 1986. Expect the classics and good wines.
france-soir.com.au

02 Pellegrini's, CBD: Virtually unchanged since opening in 1954, this family-run espresso bar has a place in the heart of all Melburnians. Coffee culture may have evolved but there's no replicating the mid-century ambiance here.
+ 61 (0)3 9662 1885

03 Abla's, Carlton: Long before Middle Eastern food became trendy, Abla Amad was warming hearts with her delicious home-style Lebanese fare and abundant Arabic hospitality. Open since 1979, Abla's really is a living treasure.
ablas.com.au

04 Supper Inn, CBD: A haven for hungry night owls and off-duty hospitality-industry workers, what this Chinatown stalwart lacks in interior design it makes up for with its food. Try the suckling pig – it's legendary.
+ 61 (0)3 9663 4759

05 Babka, Fitzroy: Bringing happiness to people via artisan baked goods since the mid-1990s, this quaint eastern European-accented patisserie is a comforting throwback to simpler times. Go for the borscht, stay for the tarte tartin.
+ 61 (0)3 9416 0091

6
Epocha, Carlton
Step back in time

In the face of relentless change, Epocha proves that there's still a place for the holy trinity of great food, consistency and proper hospitality. Housed in a two-storey Victorian terrace house overlooking Carlton Gardens, it may look like a charming old-world restaurant but it has a decidedly family feel (and even does a Sunday roast).

The menu offers polished takes on European food where simplicity is key (think steak tartare, burrata with broad beans and lemon, and pan-fried pork chop with cider and chard). Say yes to the wine recommendations and cheese trolley.
49 Rathdowne Street, 3053
+61 (0)3 9036 4949
epocha.com.au

7
Moroccan Soup Bar,
Fitzroy North
Veg out

Owner Hana Assafiri opened the doors of this vegetarian mecca in 1998 and little has changed since. The menu is still recited by all-female staff, you still can't book (arrive at 18.00 or prepare to queue) and the chickpea bake remains a comfort-food favourite. Sure, there's no meat or booze but when home-style Moroccan fare is this good, you won't care.

Decorated in North African style, the business runs on a spirit of generosity and free-flowing mint tea – like a warm embrace from an Arabic aunt who wants to make sure you have enough to eat. For lunch, try Assafiri's Moroccan Deli-cacy in Brunswick.
183 St Georges Road, 3068
+61 (0)3 9482 4240
moroccansoupbar.com.au

Must-try
Yellow tail kingfish pancetta with lemon oil from Bar Lourinhã, CBD
Icon status has been bestowed on this classic (it's been on the menu for more than 10 years) at charming Iberian-inspired Bar Lourinhã. Cured in salt and spice and finished with lemon oil and fresh thyme leaves, it's simplicity at its best.
barlourinha.com.au

8

French Saloon, CBD
Say cheese

Journeys down a lane and up a rickety old staircase are typically rewarded with good things in Melbourne and this handsome first-floor bistro is no exception. Like so many of the city's favourite venues, French Saloon feels like it's been around forever – timber floorboards, vaulted ceilings and a sweeping zinc bar bring character to the airy, loft-like dining room.

The modern European menu features exemplary seafood (oysters, caviar and sea urchin blini), in-house dry-aged steaks, serious farmhouse cheeses and a knockout wine list. Be sure to add downstairs sibling Kirk's Wine Bar to your itinerary too.
1F, 46 Hardware Lane, 3000
+61 (0)3 9600 2142
frenchsaloon.com

10
Jinda Thai, Abbotsford
Turn up the heat

Tucked away down a nondescript alley, this is one of Melbourne's best-kept, cheap-eats secrets. For lovers of serious Thai food (read: regional, not shy with the heat), this bustling warehouse-style space takes things up a huge notch from the usual cheap-and-cheerful standbys.

Rustic Thai interiors are the first surprise; the second is the flavour-packed modern Thai menu, which has the kind of complexity and sophistication usually reserved for high-end venues inspired by the country. Start with the marinated *mu ping* (pork skewers) then opt for the chilli-flecked deep-fried fish with green apple, lime and coriander salad – it's a winner.
1-7 Ferguson Street, 3067
+61 (0)3 9419 5899

9
Tipo 00, CBD
Pasta la vista

Melbourne thought it knew good pasta, then Tipo arrived on the scene in 2014: an instant classic that proved a great plate of simple Italian will never go out of style. The best bit? It took a non-Italian to do it. Greek-Australian chef-owner Andreas Papadakis has raised the bar with produce-driven dishes that are both restrained and wonderfully complex. And his switched-on staff demonstrate that hospitality is alive and well.

Highlights include the locally made burrata with crumbed aubergine and the spaghettini with red mullet, saffron and fennel. Whatever you choose, round things off with Tipomisù Papadakis, an update on the classic tiramisu.
361 Little Bourke Street, 3000
+61 (0)3 9942 3946
tipo00.com.au

⑪

HuTong Dumpling Bar City, CBD
China in your hand

Dumplings are "a thing" in Melbourne – usually with BYO beer and especially on Friday nights. Although highly decorated international players have joined the city's dumpling fray, this Chinatown stalwart still leads the pack when it comes to textbook handmade XLB (*xiao long bao*), the delicate and fragrant Shanghai-style soup dumplings with pork.

The slender, three-storey space won't win any design or service awards but that's not the point. What you're here for is authentic Shanghainese food and a few "long necks" of Tsing Tao before being shooed out the door and on to your next destination.
14-16 Market Lane, 3000
+61 (0)3 9650 8128
hutong.com.au

On the market
—

Outside Queen Victoria Market (which dates back to 1878) are fresh produce, flowers and bric-a-brac, while inside are cheesemongers, coffee merchants and more. Hungry? Make like a local and snack on bratwurst, *börek* pastries and Spanish doughnuts.
qvm.com.au

12

Anchovy, Richmond
Ladies' day

Bridge Road was once a place for cheap fashion and, while the outlets have mostly gone, it's still an unlikely spot for some of the city's best eating. But at Anchovy, that's part of the charm. Ahead of her first solo outing, chef-owner Thi Le earned her stripes at some of the country's best fine-diners.

The menu's Southeast Asian influences may seem familiar but the food is far from traditional. Beautiful produce takes everything up a notch and Le's creativity carries into dishes such as Wagyu carpaccio with wild garlic *mam nem* (fermented-fish sauce) and perilla. Dare to try the cheese and Vegemite tempura.
338 Bridge Road, 3121
+61 (0)3 9428 3526
anchovy.net.au

14
Babu Ji, St Kilda
Spice things up

Melbourne's wave of Indian migration in the 2000s resulted in a blossoming Indian culinary movement. Babu Ji was one of the pioneers and, while its founders have gone on to bigger things (opening Babu Ji in New York), the hometown hero is doing great stuff under its new custodians.

It's Indian food but not as you know it: the flavours are vibrant, produce well-sourced and technique polished. Start with street-food options such as the Uttar Pradesh-style *dahi kabab* – hung-yoghurt croquettes with roasted garlic and green chilli, finished with beetroot. Thirsty? There's a neat wine offer and a help-yourself beer fridge.
4-6 Grey Street, 3182
+61 (0)3 9534 2447
babuji.com.au

🅑
Gazi, CBD
Share and share alike

For a city with one of the biggest Greek communities outside of Athens, Melbourne sure took its time dragging Hellenic cuisine into the 21st century. The turning point was when acclaimed young chef George Calombaris turned his back on molecular gastronomy to modernise the food of his paternal ancestors – and boy, was it worth the wait.

Needless to say, Melbourne went crazy for it and the chef's delicious Greek fare now dots the city at a growing number of venues. Gazi has big flavours, generous portions and plenty of buzz. Set menus offer great value and choice – they're designed to be shared and guaranteed to delight.
2 Exhibition Street, 3000
+61 (0)3 9207 7444
gazirestaurant.com.au

⑮
Tahina, Northcote
Word on the street

It's hard to know what's more addictive at this Israeli street-food bolthole: the transcendent, aromatic falafel (crisp on the outside, pillowy soft on the inside) or the hypnotic pull of watching smooth-moving Tel Aviv-born chef-owner Roy Sassonkin weave his culinary magic to a soundtrack of booming hip-hop.

Sassonkin did time in some of Melbourne's top kitchens before striking out on his own in 2015 to give Northcote residents a taste of his homeland. His classical training is evident in the way that even the simplest salad is elevated to manna status, with produce and seasoning always on the money. Sassonkin's *shakshuka* (eggs poached in a tomato sauce) – made from his father's recipe – will make you rethink the Middle East staple for good.
223 High Street, 3070
+61 (0)3 9972 1479
tahinabar.com

16

Rumi, Brunswick East
No holding back

Thanks to the vision of young Melbourne chefs whose parents and grandparents emigrated from Italy, Greece, Vietnam and Lebanon, the city is now home to modern takes on their cuisines. Lebanese-Australian Joseph Abboud was a forerunner of the modern Middle Eastern movement here and has caused countless diners to succumb to the charms of the Levant.

A relaxed and welcoming neighbourhood favourite, Rumi encourages shared feasting and suspension of restraint – especially when it comes to standouts such as the slow-roasted lamb shoulder or the fried cauliflower with currants and pine nuts.
*116 Lygon Street, 3057
+61 (0)3 9388 8255
rumirestaurant.com.au*

Lee Ho Fook, CBD
Full-on flavour

Regardless of your heritage, Chinese food is a big deal in Melbourne but never has it been as compelling and downright addictive as it is at this new-school, neon-lit laneway diner. With a fanbase that includes restaurant critics, international chefs and lovers of traditional Chinese food, chef Victor Liong's "new-style Chinese cuisine" is a flavour bomb-dropping merger of two cultures: the discipline of his classic European culinary training and traditional Chinese ingredients.

The resulting recipes are relentlessly delicious. The lunchtime bar menu is all hits: Sichuan pepper-studded *dan dan* noodles with pork mince is a must-eat, as is the Chongqing fried chicken with garlic and chilli, especially when paired with an ice-cold local Sample Pale Ale.
*11-15 Duckboard Place, 3000
+61 (0)3 9077 6261
leehofook.com.au*

18
MoVida Next Door, CBD
Brilliant bites

MoVida's Spanish culinary revolution came at a time when an authentic take on the cuisine was foreign to Melburnians. Today Barcelona-born chef-patron Frank Camorra's trio of MoVida venues continues to prove there's much to explore in Iberian food and wine.

More bar-like than the neighbouring flagship, MoVida Next Door has an elbow-to-elbow atmosphere. Perch at the bar for aperitifs and tapas or settle in for extended snacking on seafood-leaning plates backed by an excellent Spanish and Australian wine list. For tapas and vermouth on tap, visit Camorra's bodega-style Bar Tini (two doors up).

1 Hosier Lane, 3000
+61 (0)3 9663 3038
movida.com.au

Fine-dining favourites

01 Attica, Ripponlea:
Though born in New Zealand, Ben Shewry has perhaps done more to elevate native Australian produce and tell a coherent story about regional cuisine than any other Australian chef. Consistently garnering widespread international acclaim, his menu is both an education and a delight.
attica.com.au

02 Cutler & Co, Fitzroy:
Perhaps the most "Melbourne" of the city's fine-dining venues, Andrew McConnell's flagship does effortless sophistication with aplomb. The contrast of the gritty location and the polished interiors helps, as do the inspired seasonal dishes from chef Chris Watson. We suggest ordering the tasting menu with matching wines.
cutlerandco.com.au

03 Vue de Monde, CBD:
Perched on the 55th floor, high above the city and with killer views from the bay to the city's fringes, this elegant salon cocoons diners in what is a truly immersive degustation dining experience. Native produce abounds, the service is exemplary and the wine list is stellar.
vuedemonde.com.au

19
Cicciolina, St Kilda
Food porn

Bayside St Kilda periodically lapses in and out of fashion yet glimpses of its bohemian soul thankfully still endure. Filled with regulars (and the occasional rock star) this understated and much-loved neighbourhood stalwart has been quietly unstoppable since the 1990s.

Food here (reliably excellent European-inspired classics) plays more of a support role to the moodily lit dining room's buzz, which is elevated by terrific service and the flow of great Australian and European wines. Don't fear the no-bookings policy in the evenings; a quiet booth in the back bar is just the spot for a pre-dinner negroni.
130 Acland Street, 3182
+61 (0)3 9525 3333
cicciolina.com.au

Want some?

20
Embla, CBD
Wine and dine

Many Melbourne restaurants are actually helmed by super-talented Kiwis, one of whom is chef Dave Verheul, who left Michelin-starred spots in London to open The Town Mouse (sadly now closed) here in 2013. Embla arrived in 2015 and, while it might call itself a wine bar, its food is as sophisticated as that served at any fine diner. Savvy regulars come for good vibes, great tunes and natural wines, while Verheul's technique-driven approach coaxes magic out of even the humblest ingredients.
122 Russell Street, 3000
+61 (0)3 9654 5923
embla.com.au

Food shops
Bag and buy

1
Blackhearts & Sparrows, Fitzroy
Hone your craft

With an ethos of democratising wine and an eye for the good stuff, this indie booze merchant is a hub for inner-city oenophiles and anyone keen to upgrade their drinks knowledge beyond the usual big names. Blackhearts & Sparrows is known for its top-notch service and a tailored approach to each of its neighbourhood shops.

With close to 1,000 wines in stock, there's a vague risk of being overwhelmed but the thoroughly approachable staff are trained to help you narrow down your options based on the styles you like. There are orange wines, old vintages and obscure regional labels, plus craft Australian beers, ciders and spirits.
123 Smith Street, 3065
+61 (0)3 9415 8092
blackheartsandsparrows.com.au

Pidapipó, Carlton
Ice cream of the crop

Ice cream makes everything
better and at this sunny
gelateria it's hard not to smile.
Gelato rule number one:
always trust a *gelataio* who
keeps their products in *pozzetti*
– the old-school containers
with stainless-steel lids that
enclose the goods in little
refrigerated wells. It's a
clear mark of quality, care
and freshness. Rule number
two: take a stroll with your
purchase – leafy Lygon Street
is perfect for it.

Owned by Lisa Valmorbida
(*pictured*) and her brother
Jamie – whose family also
owns King & Godfree, the
130-year-old grocery next door
– Pidapipó is popular for good
reason: its fresh gelato is made
daily, using quality ingredients
and striking a welcome
balance between tradition and
creativity. Look out for flavours
such as rose and honey nougat
or ricotta, cannoli and nutella.
299 Lygon Street, 3053
+61 (0)3 9347 4596

Spring Street Grocer, CBD
Cheese, please

It's almost disingenuous to
call this place a grocer. Yes,
it has a wonderful range of
fresh organic produce, house-
cured charcuterie, beautifully
packaged pantry-fillers and
restaurant-quality, take-home
meals but that's not all.

Out front is a traditional
Italian gelateria, while in the
back of the shop there's a
little window that dispenses
excellent takeaway lunches.
The real treat is in the
basement: a speciality cheese
cave, with its own maturing
room and the very best local
and international cheeses.
Experienced cheesemongers
are on hand to guide you
through the selection.
157 Spring Street, 3000
+61 (0)3 9639 0335
springstreetgrocer.com.au

4

Baker D Chirico, Carlton
Freshly baked

Supplying Melbourne's top restaurants, as well as a devout band of in-house regulars, artisan baker Daniel Chirico (pronounced "kirri-co") produces what many consider to be the city's finest sourdough. The good news is that the magic doesn't stop there: Chirico has long been famed for brilliant pastries, biscotti and savoury pies too.

Perhaps the true cult favourites are his custard-filled, sugar-dusted *bomboloni* (Italian doughnuts) – sweet orbs of pure delight that will have you immediately negotiating your way back in line to buy another. Seasonal offerings such as the hot-cross buns, panettone and panforte require an eagle eye and an early start (they sell out fast), while the gorgeously packaged *torrone* (nougat) makes for a perfect gift or take-home treat.

178 Faraday Street, 3053
+61 (0)3 9349 3445
bakerdchirico.com.au

Must-try
Fondue grilled cheese sandwich from Maker & Monger, South Yarra
Internationally recognised cheesemonger Anthony Femia's version of the classic snack uses Comté, Swiss gruyère, diced shallots and garlic on sourdough. But the secret is in the subtle addition of white wine.
makerandmonger.com.au

5

Lune Croissanterie, Fitzroy
Flaking out

Lining up for a Lune has
become less of a weekend sport
since siblings Kate and Cam
Reid upped stumps from a
shoebox-sized shopfront in
Elwood to their current HQ.
The cult of the Lune croissant
is well documented so it can be
tempting to wonder why all the
fuss. But forget the cynicism:
just go and try the product.

Kate learned the ropes of
traditional French patisserie
at the renowned Du Pain et
des Idées boulangerie in Paris
so it's safe to say she brings
precision and authenticity to
her craft. You can eat in (with
coffee), take away or book
"The Lune Lab" experience:
a three-course pastry flight
with a seat at the private bar.
119 Rose Street, 3065
+61 (0)3 9419 2320
lunecroissanterie.com

Drinks
Raising the bar

❷
Romeo Lane, CBD
Love affair

In a laneway just off Bourke Street, lit by the rouge glow of the Pellegrini's neon sign, is one of Melbourne's tiniest but most charming cocktail bars. All dark wood, mood lighting and vintage crystal glassware, Romeo may be modest in size but it's big on romance.

The delightfully inventive drinks menu changes regularly but if there's something you're hankering for just ask – the staff here know classic cocktails inside-out and will happily concoct something special for you. It's best suited to lone wolves or cosy twosomes, and the soundtrack of crackly jazz and swampy blues adds to the old-world mood.
1A Crossley Street, 3000
+61 (0)4 5767 3647
romeolane.com.au

❶
Longsong, CBD
Rocking horse

The thing Melburnians seem to love most about this strikingly handsome Chinatown bar is that it's actually not very "Melbourne". Housed in a century-old former horse stables, the space has the kind of lofty proportions and breezy-yet-sophisticated air more common to an upscale bar in Bangkok or Seminyak.

Cocktails are a big focus here and the setting certainly encourages ordering more than one. Start with a classic Eastside – made here with Melbourne Gin Company dry gin, cucumber and lime – or choose from a local riff on the spritz theme with the Floral & Bitter, which pairs gin and rose water with Australian bush vermouth. Need snacks? Chef David Moyle's bar menu will take care of your appetite – plump for the skewers cooked over coal.
40-44 Little Bourke Street, 3000
+61 (0)3 9653 1611
longsong.com.au

So that's why they call it Bitter!

3

Heartbreaker, CBD
Open heart

If it's a boozy, raucous
night out (or just a curious
observance of the regulars
having one) on the cards,
Michael Madrusan's good-time
dive bar is the only address
you'll need. Madrusan earned
his stripes at New York's Milk
& Honey, Little Branch and
Please Don't Tell before
opening speakeasy-like The
Everleigh in Fitzroy (also
a favourite of ours). It's safe
to say that the man knows his
way around a Boston shaker.

With its rock'n'roll
jukebox, scarlet neon and
03.00 license, Heartbreaker is
a wonderfully louche antidote
to the buttoned-up earnestness
you'll find elsewhere. The
main point is that it's a whole
lot of fun. When the hunger
inevitably sets in just saunter
next door to Connie's Pizza
for a quick fix in the form of
a New York-style slice.
234A Russell Street, 3000
+61 (0)3 9041 0856
heartbreakerbar.com.au

④

Stomping Ground, Collingwood
Traditional tipples

In the late 1800s, Collingwood and Abbotsford were the hub of the city's beer industry. Most of the breweries have long been demolished or converted into apartments but this newcomer has brought the tradition back to its old stomping ground (hence the name).

The brewery and beer hall has up to 20 beers on tap and a big range to take away. Divided into categories that loosely translate as "drinkable", "complex" and "bold", the beer menu includes Belgian wheat beer, French saison, IPA and English brown ale. For a comprehensive education, try the "mixed six" – your choice of six 100-millilitre samples.
100 Gipps Street, 3066
+61 (0)3 9415 1944
stompingground.beer

⑤

The Napier Hotel, Fitzroy
Be yourself

Fitzroy is home to some of Melbourne's most beloved old boozers, many of which have retained their charm despite the galloping gentrification. Not only does that make the area a great place to dive into Victorian craft beers, it's also somewhere you can sneak a glimpse of the other side of Melbourne – where the city is happily embracing its Aussie-ness and just being itself.

Opened in 1866, this pub draws crowds of all ages for midweek knock-offs, front-bar banter and fireside dinners (the pub fare is legendary). Expect about 20 beers on tap. To make like a regular, order a "pot" (a certain size of beer) and settle in for some footy on the TV.
210 Napier Street, 3065
+61 (0)3 9419 4240
thenapierhotel.com

Wine list

With its first vines planted in the mid-1800s, Victoria's wine industry is long established but today's talented winemakers really know how to showcase their region's distinctive terroir. From flinty Henty riesling and elegant Gippsland pinot noir to Yarra Valley sparkling and Rutherglen fortified, you'll find plenty to explore here. Don't worry if you run out of time: you can always pick up a few bottles to take home with you. Here's our recommended shopping list.

01 **Henty riesling by Crawford River**
crawfordriverwines.com
02 **Yarra Valley pinot noir by The Wanderer**
wandererwines.com
03 **Heathcote nebbiolo refosco by Little Reddie**
littlereddie.com.au
04 **Geelong chardonnay by Bannockburn**
bannockburnvineyards.com
05 **Beechworth chardonnay by Giaconda**
giaconda.com.au
06 **Gippsland pinot noir by William Downie**
williamdownie.com.au
07 **Macedon Ranges pinot noir from Curly Flat**
curlyflat.com
08 **King Valley pinot grigio by Pizzini**
pizzini.com.au
09 **Grampians shiraz by Mount Langi Ghiran**
langi.com.au
10 **Sunbury shiraz by Craiglee Vineyard**
craigleevineyard.com

Wine bars
A vine romance

01 02

03 04 05

06 07

08   09

10

11   12

01 — 03 Gerald's Bar, Carlton North: A rollicking neighbourhood institution filled with vintage curios, incredible wines and vintage soul on vinyl. The service is affable, the food superb and on occasion punters get to choose which wines by the glass are opened each night.
geraldsbar.com.au

04 — 07 Napier Quarter, Fitzroy: Located on one of Fitzroy's prettiest tree-lined backstreets, this is the kind of low-key but switched-on local we all wish we had. Open from breakfast until late, it comes into its own around sunset. Expect charming interiors, beautifully plated food and thoughtfully selected wines.
napierquarter.com.au

08 — 09 City Wine Shop, CBD: Elegantly lived-in, with buckets of old-world charm, this cosy wine shop-cum-bar attracts everyone from visiting French winemakers to off-duty cabinet ministers. The food is excellent and the staff know their wines so let them take the lead.
citywineshop.net.au:

10 Marion, Fitzroy: Effortlessly sleek with a killer wine list, Marion makes a great case for bypassing dinner in favour of drinks and small plates. Lean against the narrow bar with a Rutherglen fino and some native oysters before embarking on a guided vinous journey.
marionwine.com.au

11 — 12 Ramblr, South Yarra: Leading the south-side revival, this "casual fine diner" straddles the line between restaurant and wine bar. The food is excellent and the wine list champions small producers. A great spot to get to know a Heathcote fiano or Gippsland pinot.
ramblr.com.au

Retail
— Talking shop

Australia may be the spiritual home of the shopping centre and boast one of the globe's strongest e-commerce markets but Melbourne is proof that a vibrant high street lined with plucky retailers can still hold its own against the commercial titans and lure of the click-to-buy culture.

The city's villagey feel means that shoppers can find pockets of retail opportunity scattered across town, from Fitzroy's eclectic Gertrude Street and modish Smith Street in Collingwood to lengthy Lygon Street a little further west. Even the CBD – once you've bypassed the ubiquitous chain offerings and tacky tourist traps – can prove surprisingly fertile ground, with a clutch of independent shops secreted away among its laneways and arcades.

We've rounded up our favourite purveyors of products proudly sporting a "Made in Melbourne" sticker. Expect beautifully conceived spaces and snappy branding across the board: this is a city that knows how to make you part with your cash.

①
CIBI, Collingwood
Japanese gem

Meg and Zenta Tanaka (*both pictured*) combined their backgrounds in architecture, design, food and wine to open this charmingly eclectic slice of Japan on a Collingwood backstreet in 2008. The concept store is a recipe for living slowly, with good design and nourishing food as key ingredients.

"I wanted to create a space where people can pop in and be inspired or enjoy a special moment in everyday life," says Zenta. Hard-to-find *tamagoyaki* (rolled omelette) pans, woodblock-printed textiles and handcrafted knives feature among the homeware crafted by small-scale Japanese makers. The on-site café serves traditional Japanese breakfast on weekends – and don't miss sister food project Mina No Ie (*see page 29*) on nearby Peel Street.
45 Keele Street, 3066
+61 (0)3 9077 3941
shop.cibi.com.au

②

Mr Kitly, Brunswick
Kit and caboodle

Blink and you'll miss the slim
set of stairs that leads to this
combined shop, gallery and
architecture studio. Five years in
Japan galvanised Bree Claffey's
passion for ceramics and this,
paired with a desire to celebrate
artisan skills, inspired her to
establish Mr Kitly in 2010.

Despite the bustle of
Brunswick below, it's a serene
space, filled with functional and
decorative objects that focus
on craftsmanship. Think tactile
ceramics from Australia and
abroad, books on travel and
architecture, plus wood, metal
and textile goods for the home.
There's a dedicated plant room,
while monthly exhibitions
adorn the central gallery.

381 Sydney Road, 3056
+61 (0)3 9078 7357
mrkitly.com.au

3

Craft Victoria, CBD
Design minds

Founded in 1970, arts
organisation Craft has
long celebrated Australian
craftsmanship and design
through its series of exhibitions,
festivals, lectures and
workshops – and now also
via this physical shop just
off Flinders Lane. Here
you'll find the wares of the
organisation's maker members,
which range from jewellery,
ceramics and glass pieces to
textiles, furniture, sculpture
and fashion. Each item comes
with a short blurb about the
brains behind it.
Watson Place, 3000
+61 (0)3 9650 7775
craft.org.au

4

The Boroughs, Brunswick East
Form and function

Since 2007, Alasdair
MacKinnon has sought
products that are "functional,
beautiful and enduring" –
most of which come from
the surrounding creative
community – to fill his
Lygon Street enclave of
homeware and gifts. Otto &
Spike knitwear from nearby
Brunswick joins Melbourne-
made ceramics by Tara
Shackell and Leaf and
Thread, along with textiles,
stationery, books and art.
  MacKinnon also
collaborates with local makers
to shape an in-house line of tea
towels, journals, pillowcases
and even a bespoke chocolate
bar with Monsieur Truffe (*see
page 69*) two doors along.
345 Lygon Street, 3057
+61 (0)3 9388 1618
theboroughs.co

Watch this space
———

This old watch factory has
returned to its craftsmanship
roots with Captains of Industry,
housing a contemporary
jeweller, a bespoke shoemaker
and a barbershop. The on-
site café transforms into a
Prohibition-esque bar on
Friday evenings.
+61 (0)3 9670 4405

This is the life

Homeware
Part of the furniture

①
Pop & Scott, Northcote
It takes two

Poppy Lane and Scott Gibson began collaborating under their eponymous Pop & Scott brand in 2012. Today they are joined by a small team of artists and makers to create their collection of mid-century-inspired Australian design with an emphasis on traditional handicrafts.

Sustainably sourced Australian ash furniture, delicately woven lamps and signature hand-painted pots come together in the pair's Northcote workshop and showroom. The majority of their range is made on-site and joined by Pampa rugs, Anchor Ceramics and Nicolette Johnson vases in the showroom. The brand is driven by the belief that "spaces should always be inviting, products ethical, and furniture made and used for wine and cheese". We'll drink to that.
27 Hayes Street, 3070
+61 (0)474 548 194
popandscott.com

❷
Jardan, Richmond
Made in Melbourne

Walk through this expansive,
light-filled showroom and
you'll spot colours reminiscent
of the Australian landscape:
the blue of gum trees, the
pink of an outback sunset
and sea-foam green. "We
look to Europe for design
inspiration but adapt it to suit
the Australian lifestyle," says
co-owner Nick Garnham. "We
imagine what we have in our
beach house then throw in
some playful references, such
as a nod to your grandma's
hand-me-down sofa."

But Jardan's furniture –
all designed and made in
Melbourne – is anything but
old-fashioned or fusty. Expect
elegant sideboards of smooth
Tasmanian oak, sleek bedside
tables in brushed brass and,
of course, those deep-set sofas
that any granny would be
proud to own.
522 Church Street, 3121
+61 (0)3 8581 4988
jardan.com.au

❸
Modern Times, Fitzroy
Old and new

This showroom is packed
with vintage pieces of furniture
tastefully matched with
contemporary Australian art
and design objects. Husband
and wife Joel and Amy
Malin source the majority
of their wares in Europe
before bringing them back to
Melbourne to be restored by
a team of in-house experts.

While you may not have
room for a Hans J Wegner
cord armchair or 1950s Italian
velvet sofa in your carry-on,
there are plenty of luggage-
friendly purchases in the form
of ceramics, textiles, jewellery
and prints.
311 Smith Street, 3065
+61 (0)3 9913 8598
moderntimes.com.au

Home and away
───
With stock from France,
Sweden, Denmark and beyond,
Dean Angelucci's Fitzroy shop
– Angelucci 20th Century – is a
trove of imported and restored
homeware mainly from the
1950s and 1960s. Don't miss
its bespoke mid-century-style
pieces, made in the city.
angelucci.net.au

Specialist retail
One-stop shops

④

Criteria, Cremorne
Worldly wares

Established in 2014 by New
Yorker Rachael Fry (*pictured*),
Criteria carries a tight selection
of international furniture,
design and art pieces,
specialising in lighting by Big
Apple-based brands such
as Apparatus Studio, David
Weeks and Bec Brittain.

With its exposed brick walls
and artfully arranged furniture,
this capacious warehouse space
certainly feels part gallery, part
showroom and part swanky
Manhattan loft apartment.
66 Gwynne Street, 3121
+61 (0)3 9421 2636
criteriacollection.com.au

①

Azalea Flowers, South
Melbourne
Bloomin' marvellous

For Michael Pavlou (*pictured*),
flowers run in the family.
"Some of my earliest memories
are of wrapping flowers with
my aunty at the Sunday
markets," says Pavlou. In
2014, he pressed pause on a
psychology degree to open his
own flower shop in the lively
South Melbourne Market.

Here he places emphasis
on seasonality, arranging all
manner of native flowers and
foliage (and some beloved
textural exotics) into dazzling
bouquets. "There are so
many flowers and plants
endemic to Australia that no
one has seen before and I
decided to change that," he
says. As well as sourcing from
wholesale markets and direct
from farms, Pavlou also works
with growers to cultivate
specific native blooms.
*Shop 49, 322-326 Coventry
Street, 3205*
+61 (0)3 9696 4978
azaleaflowers.com.au

②

Wootten, Prahran
A lotta leather

Jess Cameron-Wootten knows a thing or two about leather. His father started making shoes in the early 1970s and Jess not only inherited his collection of tools but also his passion for the material, having since made bespoke boots for AFL stars and footwear for A-list actresses. Today he has established himself as Melbourne's go-to leather guy: Cameron-Wootten's handiwork can be found everywhere from the barista aprons at Patricia (*see page 27*) to tablet covers in the rooms at Jackalope hotel (*see page 22*).

You'll find a range of accessories and footwear available off-the-shelf but Wootten also offers a bespoke service, working with a variety of leathers including kangaroo, crocodile and barramundi. Note that the retail space is only open Thursday–Saturday.
20 Grattan Street, 3181
+61 (0)3 9510 6503
wootten.com.au

③

Tarlo & Graham, Fitzroy
Into the mix

"We put a lot of effort into creating a different retail experience" says Philip Graham, who founded this Aladdin's cave in Fitzroy with co-owner William Tarlo in 2003. "We select from a range of styles, periods and themes that interest us but all the items you find in the shop will have beauty, a touch of humour and a synergy with everything else."

Such a brief results in an eclectic offering: expect anything from natural history and scientific pieces (think taxidermy badger cosying up to a French optometrist's lamp) to art, antiques and lighting. Plus, the best window displays on the street.
202 Gertrude Street, 3065
+61 (0)3 9417 7773
tarloandgraham.com

Beauty spot
—

Aesop may now be ubiquitous but its roots lie in Melbourne. With its commitment to compelling retail spaces and focus on quality – not to mention that iconic, oft-imitated packaging – it's hard to think of a brand that better embodies the city.
aesop.com

❹

Double Monk, Fitzroy
Sole traders

Double Monk is the
brainchild of brothers Chris
and Nick Schaerf and boasts
an extensive range of shoes
by industry leaders such as
Crockett & Jones, John Lobb
and Edward Green. "Many of
the brands we stock were near
impossible to find in Australia
before we opened," says Chris.
 The plush, masculine space
features oak parquet flooring
reclaimed from a castle in
Germany while the towering
wooden shelves are accessed
by rolling ladders. At the back
of the shop you'll find a well-
stocked bar complete with
Chesterfield armchairs. Taking
your time is encouraged here –
some of the shoes on sale take
the best part of a year to make.
53 Smith Street, 3065
+61 (0)3 9417 3335
doublemonk.com

Menswear
Man to man

❶

Masons, CBD
From suits to boardshorts

Multibrand retailer Masons
is housed in a heritage-listed
Edwardian warehouse on
Flinders Lane. The polished
fit-out by Cox Architecture is
all sharp lines, Italian marble
and Japanese parquet flooring.
Black metal rails display a mix
of streetwear and sartorial
pieces from the likes of
Vivienne Westwood, Maison
Kitsuné and Slowear.
 The offering is designed
to be multi-generational:
expect to find a pair of playful
Marni boardshorts hanging
next to the sharpest suits this
side of Milan. Feeling the
fatigue of your foray down
Flinders Lane? Allow one of
the dapper staff to pour you
a whisky from the bar.
167 Flinders Lane, 3000
+61 (0)3 9380 7188
masonsofficial.com

2

Pickings & Parry, Fitzroy
Man's world

The son of a butcher, Chris Pickings (*pictured*) attributes his interest in menswear and style to growing up in the north of England under the influence of Oasis and inheriting his father's collection of vintage clothing, guitars and records. He moved to Melbourne in 2011, where he saw a gap in the market for a menswear outlet selling authentic, international heritage brands.

"I expected to find shops catering to this end of men's style but there weren't many at all – everything I wanted to buy I had to buy online," he says. The Fitzroy shop also includes a barber (*see page 128*) that offers a range of traditional grooming services.
Shop 3, 166 Gertrude Street, 3065
+61 (0)3 9417 3390
pickingsandparry.com

3
Carl Navè, CBD
Tailor made

Born into a family of Italian tailors and dressmakers, Carl Navè (*pictured*) first picked up a needle and thread at the age of six. After formalising his training at RMIT and cutting his teeth with some of the city's most prominent tailors, he opened his own studio in 2012 and now turns out his own line of made-to-measure clothes from classic business and dinner suits to a wide range of sports jackets, overcoats, tailored shirts and accessories.

Navè uses Australian wool wherever possible. "Victorian wool is some of the best in the world and I am very proud to know that my products begin and finish their journey here," he says.

2B, 190-192 Bourke Street, 3000
+61 (0)3 9972 3173
carlnave.com.au

4
The Practical Man, CBD
Good fit

This sportswear shop caters to men who like their workout clothes to be both handsome and comfortable. "We're a destination for those who want well-designed items that will last," says co-founder Brett Webster, who also runs a Pilates studio in the city. "Some of the brands we stock use the same textile mills as top-end fashion labels such as Zegna. Who says clothes for running have to be boring?"

Fashion-focused fitness buffs will find a selection that stretches beyond the ubiquitous global sports brands to include labels such as Spalwart and White Mountaineering and Parisian cult running label Satisfy. There's also a range of grooming products smartly displayed in the pegboard-clad space designed by local carpenter Chris Tomoya.

Scott Alley, 237 Flinders Lane, 3000
+61 (0)3 9654 4513
thepracticalman.com

Denim

01 **Nobody, Fitzroy:** With a factory in Thonbury, this denim giant has been synonymous with Melbourne fashion since 1999. High-quality fabrics and ethical accreditation are the bedrock of the family-run operation, which turns out organic cotton T-shirts alongside new and reused denim.
nobodydenim.com

02 **Denimsmith, Brunswick East:** Pieces from this small-batch label are made by owner Vinh Le and his team from fine Japanese denim. At the Brunswick East shop, peer past the glass divide to witness the goings on of the factory itself. The brand offers tailoring and custom fittings too.
denimsmith.com.au

03 **Service, Fitzroy:** A defunct textiles factory now houses the bricks-and-mortar retail concept of three denim brands. Neuw, Rolla's and Abrand teamed up as Threebyone collective in 2009 and have been marketing their denim from common space Service ever since.
servicedenim.com

Thank you, I grew it myself

Mixed fashion
His and hers

❶
Handsom, Fitzroy
Look and feel

Sam Rush and Henry Allum
(*pictured*) founded Handsom
in 2009, before opening this
flagship shop in 2012. "Expect
soft tailoring and relaxed
silhouettes in premium fabrics,
with an emphasis on texture
and colour," says Rush of
their small-batch, sustainably
produced collections.

Here, functional, well-
constructed items are joined
by Australia's Pared Eyewear
and Hakea Swim, as well as US
offering Malibu Sandals. Each
piece is designed in the upstairs
studio and manufactured at
ethically accredited factories
overseas. Knitwear is made
from Merino wool while yarns
are fashioned from the likes of
bamboo and hemp-cotton.
163 Gertrude Street, 3065
+61 (0)3 9078 7306
handsom-store.com

*Do these come
in another size?*

2

Bassike, CBD
Simple pleasures

For more than a decade this iconic Australian label has been seducing shoppers with its organic cotton basics. "Our design process always starts with the fabric," says Deborah Sams, who co-founded the brand with Mary Lou Ryan in 2006. The pair has always kept sustainable and ethical production front of mind, sourcing high-quality yarn from Australia, Italy and Japan.

You'll find this shop down a discrete laneway in the CBD. Inside, whitewashed brick walls act as a suitable canvas for the covetable essentials and seasonal lines comprising tailored shirts, denim, swimwear and jewellery.
1-3 Rankins Lane, 3000
+61 (0)3 8677 5702
bassike.com

3

Alpha 60, CBD
Shape shifters

This quintessential Melbourne label has been layering locals in geometric dresses and wide-legged culottes since its inception in 2003. Brother-sister duo Alex and Georgie Cleary took inspiration for the name from Jean-Luc Godard's 1965 sci-fi classic *Alphaville* and it's evident how the dystopian marvel informs their inimitable collections.

One of 12 across Australia, this heritage-listed location – designed by New York-based Jen Berean and Melbourne's Light Project – juxtaposes a classical vaulted ceiling and stained-glass windows with video projections and a central army of mannequins.
Chapter House, 195 Flinders Lane, 3000
+61 (0)3 9663 3002
alpha60.com.au

④
Incu, CBD
Near and far

Twin brothers Brian and
Vincent Wu gave up careers
in business to found Incu and
now have eight shops across
the country. This space in the
QV shopping centre houses
both men's and womenswear,
as well as accessories, from
a meticulous edit of global
brands. It's the place to go
for well-designed statement
threads, with contemporary
basics from the duo's in-
house label Incu Collection
complementing pieces by Acne
Studios, Comme des Garçons,
and Rag & Bone.

The name is a truncated
version of "Incubator",
reflecting the brothers' support
of local labels such as Dress Up,
Bellroy and Lucy Folk.
QV, Albert Coates Lane, 3000
+61 (0)3 9654 4725
incu.com

Womenswear
Feminine touch

①
Kloke, Fitzroy
Plain sailing

After each working for
notable Australian fashion
houses, couple Amy and
Adam Coombes combined
their talents to launch this
progressive label in 2011.
"Washed-back Japanese denim
and superior Merino knits are
staples," says Adam of their
scrupulously selected fabrics,
which the pair transform
into boxy jumpsuits, kimono
dresses and tie-belted trousers
in monochromatic shades.

For this Fitzroy shop,
Melbourne studio Sibling
stripped back the Victorian-
era interior to its original
form, re-shaping a calming
retail space with touches of
local ash, concrete, limed
floorboards and custom-made
copper clothing racks.
270 Brunswick Street, 3065
+61 (0)3 9078 6600
kloke.com.au

2

Monk House Design, CBD
Good things, small packages

Roula Tzidras has an eye for small-batch local labels that "do what they do to an exceptional level, with high consideration of design and ethical production". That's been her ethos since opening the original Brunswick East flagship in 2005.

At this more recent CBD shop, her collection of both progressive and practical clothing, shoes and jewellery sits within a playful minimalist interior that's framed by an opulent heritage milieu. A handful of global names fill the gaps between Melbourne's Verner, Mirador, Dress Up and Pageant. As do pieces from the in-house brand, which are made in Melbourne in small batches.
4 Driver Lane, 3000
+61 (0)3 9654 2531
monkhousedesign.com

3

Kuwaii, Brunswick
Go slow

Kristy Barber founded Kuwaii as an antidote to fast fashion. Her considered approach yields well-made dresses, jumpsuits, culottes and T-shirts in painterly hues that mosey from staple to statement. "Every Kuwaii piece is designed, made and sold within 15km of our Brunswick flagship," says Barber of the decidedly small footprint.

Just two makers carry out the precise tailoring, meaning runs are often limited to 10 to 20 per garment. Footwear is handcrafted in nearby Abbotsford while fabrics are sourced directly from mills in Italy, France and Japan. You'll find shop number two in Cathedral Arcade in the CBD.
37-39 Glenlyon Road, 3056
+61 (0)3 9380 5731
kuwaii.com.au

④

Obus, CBD
Prints charming

Kylie Zerbst has been creating contemporary silhouettes in playful prints since founding this highly regarded label in 1998. Zerbst is the artist behind each collection's vivid patterns and, with small production runs, dedicated followers are guaranteed an original, distinctive mien.

Sustainability is held at the fore – with fabrics knitted from bamboo, tencel and organic cotton – and pieces are made locally where possible (clothing in Melbourne, swimwear in Sydney and nail polish in Queensland). This Cathedral Arcade space joins outposts in Fitzroy, Brunswick East and Northcote.
*Shop 5, Cathedral Arcade,
37 Swanston Street, 3000
+61 (0)3 9639 5801
obus.com.au*

More womenswear

01 **Búl, citywide:** The contemporary tailoring and clean lines of this Melbourne-born label are inspired by travel. Since 2010, designer Virginia Martin has added shoes, eyewear and accessories to her repertoire and now oversees five shops in Melbourne alone.
bul.com.au

02 **Elk, Preston:** Husband-and-wife team Marnie Goding and Adam Koniaras have steadily grown this Preston-based label since launching in 2004. Expect biannual collections of clothing, accessories, leather goods and shoes, which are ethically made by small manufacturers both locally and overseas.
elkaccessories.com/au

03 **Limb, Fitzroy:** This young label has been making waves with its trans-seasonal slips and tailored outerwear since launching in late 2015. Each collection is made in Melbourne and the Fitzroy flagship hosts a melange of pieces by other small-scale Australian designers.
limbthelabel.com

Three's a crowd
—
No Order Market is one of the city's most avant garde retail offerings. Split into thirds, the shared space is home to multi-brand retailer Shifting Worlds, bedding and leisurewear brand Suku Home and French-Danish label Baserange.
noordermarket.com

❶

Happy Valley, Collingwood
Change of scene

After 15 years in the music industry (he ran Fitzroy's Polyester Records shop for a decade and founded his own independent label) followed by a brief spell managing a pub, Chris Crouch decided that his true passion lay in retail and established Happy Valley in 2013. "It took me 18 months to find the right shop," he says. "I was more interested in the perfect space than the perfect location."

It turns out he succeeded on both accounts, managing to secure a prime spot on Collingwood's vibrant Smith Street. Crouch's shelves are lined with a thoughtful edit of books and gifts, many of which come from local designers. Naturally, the vinyl collection is also on point.
294 Smith Street, 3066
+61 (0)3 9077 8509
happyvalleyshop.com

3

Perimeter Books, Thornbury
By the book

Dan Rule founded this
handsome bookshop with
his wife Justine Ellis in 2011,
prompted by what they saw
as an under-representation
of independent international
publishers in Australia. "Our
intention was to create a kind
of 'window' into contemporary
art and photography-related
publishing practices in Europe,
Japan and North America,"
says Rule. Expect books, zines
and periodicals covering a
wide range of subjects from
art, culture and design to
architecture and urbanism.
748 High Street, 3071
+61 (0)3 9484 8101
perimeterbooks.com

2

Northside Records, Fitzroy
Making music

Founded by Chris Gill
(*pictured*) in 2002, Northside
Records is Melbourne's
go-to for the snappiest in
new and used vinyl. Gill's
weekly radio show *Get Down*
on Melbourne's community
station 3RRR sets the tone
for the shop, which is packed
with funk, soul, hip-hop and
disco, as well as cuts from
classic labels such as Bluenote
and Prestige.

Gill believes that it's
important to invest in the local
music culture, so you'll find
plenty of cuts by Melbourne
artists such as The Bamboos
and Cookin' on 3 Burners,
as well as stacks of 45s from
soul label Hope Street. Gill
also plugs gigs on his website,
saying that "there's no point
pushing new soul and funk
music if you can't engage
with it."
236 Gertrude Street, 3065
+61 (0)3 9417 7557
northsiderecords.com.au

4

Readings Books, Carlton
Writers' block

Mark Rubbo bought Readings Books in 1976 and, over the past four decades, has turned it into a Carlton institution. The towering shelves stock a range of genres but aficionados come for the literary fiction, art, design, travel and music titles.

Independent publishers and literary magazines are well represented and complemented by a colourful programme of weekly events that include book signings and poetry readings. The new children's bookshop next door features a mural by artist and author Marc Martin.
309 Lygon Street, 3053
+61 (0)3 9347 6633
readings.com.au/carlton

Page turner
—
The arrival of Magnation came at a time when many purveyors of print had banned customers from browsing pages in store. This dedicated magazine-seller encouraged it and, in the process, attracted a loyal and long-standing clientele.
magnation.com

5

Dutch Vinyl, Abbotsford
Safe and sound

Sourcing vinyl from trips to the Netherlands and beyond, Mark Reuten has been assembling one of Melbourne's best selections of quality collectibles since 2016. His smart, homely shop houses vinyl in wooden bins – large letters printed on rollout drawers will help you find what you are looking for. Genres range from rare jazz, soul and blues to surf, rock and nineties techno.

Other tricks up Reuten's record sleeves include becoming the only Australian distributor of the quality (and affordable) Blake plastic sleeves and being the proud owner of a Clearaudio Sonic record cleaner, ensuring his discs have the purest sound possible.
269 Johnston Street, 3067
+61 (0)3 481 882 219
dutchvinyl.com.au

Things we'd buy
—— Made in Melbourne

Shopping may be serious business in this city but Melbourne's retail offering is far from staid: whether it's ceramics embellished with native botanicals, socks emblazoned with trams or a cuddly kangaroo that you're after, we've got your top take-homes covered.

We've picked out a couple of bottles of local plonk – and a whisky distilled in Port Melbourne – to jazz up your drinks cabinet, sourced some smart threads courtesy of our favourite homegrown talents and found a set of snappy gardening tools for the green-fingered. Of course, we've also garnered coffee in its many guises (along with all the associated paraphernalia), from beans and cups to espresso martinis and coffee body scrubs – and even a barista's apron if you want to take things to the next level. Let the fun begin.

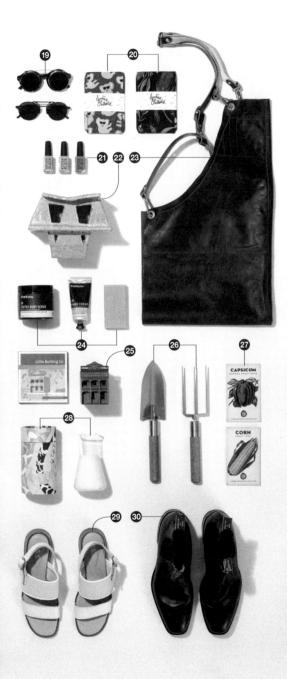

01 Edwina Bolger kangaroo from Craft Victoria *craft.org.au*
02 Alma & Co cityscape cushion from The Shelley Panton Store *shelleypanton.com*
03 Lafitte tram socks from The Shelley Panton Store *shellypanton.com*
04 Coffee by Seven Seeds *sevenseeds.com.au*
05 Monsieur Truffe chocolate from The Boroughs *theboroughs.co*
06 *Speciality Coffee Melbourne* from Readings Books *readings.com.au*
07 Takeawei sun mug from Craft Victoria *craft.org.au*
08 KeepCup from Happy Valley *happyvalleyshop.com*
09 Mr Smith haircare products from Prophecy *prophecyhair.com.au*
10 Apiary Made jelly bush honey from Melbournalia *melbournalia.com.au*
11 Melbourne Martini espresso martini from Dan Murphy's *danmurphys.com.au*
12 Angus & Celeste ceramics from Wilkins and Kent *wilkinsandkent.com*
13 Ghostwares ceramics from Nature Boy Nrth *natureboynrth.com*
14 A Rodda Beechworth chardonnay from City Wine Shop *citywineshop.net.au*
15 Mac Forbes pinot noir from City Wine Shop *citywineshop.net.au*
16 Maidenii vermouth from Blackhearts & Sparrows *blackheartsandsparrows.com.au*
17 Starward whisky from Blackhearts & Sparrows *blackheartsandsparrows.com.au*
18 Hot chocolate by Mörk *morkchocolate.com.au*
19 Dot Dot sunglasses from The Cool Hunter Store *thecoolhunter.net*
20 Julie White socks from The Boroughs Store *theboroughs.co*
21 Kester Black nail polish from Kiosk *kiosktheshop.com*

22 McCraith House ceramic
sculpture by Natalie Rosin
from Jardan *jardan.com.au*
23 Leather apron by Wootten
wootten.com.au
24 Thankyou cosmetics
from Coles *coles.com.au*
25 Little Building Co model
house from Happy Valley
happyvalleyshop.com

26 Grafa garden tools from
Mr Kitly *mrkitly.com.au*
27 Heritage seeds from Little
Veggie Patch
littleveggiepatchco.com.au
28 Alchemy Produx candle
from Plyroom *plyroom.com.au*
29 Post Sole Studio sandals
from FME Apparel
fmeapparel.com.au

30 Classic boots by RM Williams
rmwilliams.com.au
31 *The Australian Ugliness* by
Robin Boyd from Readings Books
readings.com.au
32 Tote bag by Gorman
gormanshop.com.au
33 T-shirt by A.BCH *abch.world*
34 Menswear by Handsom
handsom-store.com

10 essays
—— Get the
measure of the city

Why thank
you, I think
it's a fine
story too

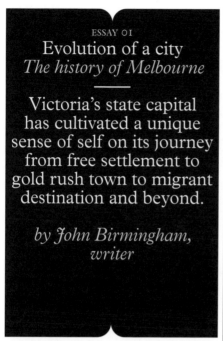

ESSAY 01

Evolution of a city
The history of Melbourne

Victoria's state capital has cultivated a unique sense of self on its journey from free settlement to gold rush town to migrant destination and beyond.

by John Birmingham, writer

In one of the great disappointments of Australian history, the most Gotham of all Antipodean cities was initially known as Batmania, until some short-sighted idiot renamed it Melbourne. That idiot was the governor of New South Wales, sucking up to the British prime minister William Lamb, who was also known as the 2nd Viscount Melbourne. Exactly what the 2nd Viscount thought of lending his name to a handful of mouldering tents, bark huts and shallow holes in which to poo is not recorded. But Melbourne it was.

Settled by free men – or stolen from the people of the Wurundjeri, Boonwurrung and Wathaurong tribes, to be completely honest about it –

Melbourne enjoyed thinking of itself as something a little bit special. It was, after all, no mere prison camp like Sydney. But nor was it large, wealthy or strategically significant to the British Empire… like Sydney. Global capital flowed into and out of the continent via that thriving entrepôt on the warm shores of the Pacific to the north – and with that wealth came power and prominence, despite the convict stain.

The southern metropolis might never have got over its resentment of trailing behind Sydney's monetised gulag were it not for the gold rush of the 1850s. In three years, everything flipped. A remote dependency gained worldwide fame. The population exploded, wealth grew exponentially – and with it the port and city closest to the diggings. Modern Melbourne, the old-money capital, a grand vision of Paris remade on the far side of the world, was a reboot of the earlier concept of a freely settled city but this time done with an unlimited budget and a huge international cast.

For a few short years all the money in the world seemed to flood through the streets and with it came pioneers, chancers, fortune seekers and hundreds of thousands of hopeful migrants. The gold petered out but the wealth remained and by then it had so supercharged the economy of Melbourne that the rest of the country would be another century catching up. The migrants kept coming too, with waves of Italians, Greeks and other continental outcasts pouring in after the Second World War, bringing with them the refined sensibilities of Europe.

Grand boulevards, spacious parks, elegant terraced inner suburbs and hugely serious public architecture conjured a vision of the old world in the new. Lacking Sydney's impossibly beautiful harbour and beaches, coastal cliffs and hinterland ranges, the flat monotonous plains of Melbourne instead presented a blank tablet on which the city's nouveau riche could spend their fortunes on world-building at scale. To this day the city's internal life remains vastly superior to any pretenders or challengers.

"Modern Melbourne was a reboot of the concept of a freely settled city but this time done with an unlimited budget and a huge international cast"

Whether the interiority is physical or otherwise, everything that happens within – be it the built environment, the city's nightlife, its artistic realms, its bars, cafés, clubs and restaurants, its libraries and galleries, all of these expressions and domains of the inner life – is more finely developed in Melbourne than any other Australian city.

Sydney eventually took back its role at the nation's economic centre. Brisbane's growth and proximity to Asia-Pacific financial centres will see it eclipse the Victorian capital's population and eventually its wealth and consequence. But as much as a city can know its own mind, Melbourne knows that it doesn't care. The quality of urban life is not measured purely in hard data but also by less concrete metrics. Melbourne knows it's the best of places. If only it had the best of names. Batmania forever. — (M)

Fun facts
—
01 Happy little Vegemite
Port Melbourne is the only place in the world making Vegemite.
02 Green light
Melbourne installed the country's first traffic lights in 1928.
03 Formerly known as
The Yarra was so polluted in the 1880s that the city was dubbed Smelbourne.

ABOUT THE WRITER: Australian writer John Birmingham was a contributing editor at *Rolling Stone* for a decade before winning the National Award for Non-Fiction. He lives on a high hill with two dogs and some other family stragglers.

ESSAY 02

Creek legend
The rebirth of Merri Creek

Fifty years ago it was an overgrown and polluted magnet for lost souls. Today, Merri Creek has been rehabilitated as a haven for the region's flora and fauna.

by Myfanwy Jones, writer

I grew up in a cream weatherboard in Melbourne's inner north, a short drive from the city centre. The house backed onto the Merri Creek. You could scale the woven-wire fence and tumble straight into overgrown rye and wild fennel, into a different quality of air, light, sound, smell and texture.

The creek in the 1970s was a wild and unkempt place and my sisters and I were the same. Always barefoot, we roamed freely. We climbed the generous arms of the weeping willows that lined the banks, rolled like sausages down grassy slopes and wandered up wastewater pipes, hands and feet braced against porous concrete. We lost and found things along the creek – mostly ourselves.

I remember the buzz of March flies and dragonflies. Sunbathing tiger snakes. Scampering water rats. Warbling magpies. The sour stink of refuse dumped by factories upstream. Through most of the 20th century the creek was put to heavy industrial use, the water greasy and full of heavy metals.

We observed odd human behaviour – urban waterways magnetise lost souls. A bearded man who lived rough and scared. A small woman with a large dog and ghoulish make-up. A man who always crinkled like a packet of crisps – what the hell did he have under that sweatshirt? One night someone ran amok with a gun – we hid indoors. Sir David Attenborough might comment sagely on this pulsing human activity: the creek was a sanctuary for all creatures.

Decades later, I find myself walking the banks of the Merri. I did try other suburbs and worked abroad for a couple of years, only to arrive at the beginning, in another cream weatherboard house across the footbridge from my childhood home. My sons have grown up on the same ribbon of water though their

"We lost and found things along the creek – mostly ourselves. I remember the buzz of March flies and dragonflies. Sunbathing tiger snakes"

upbringings and the modern-day Merri are ostensibly tamer. My generation keeps closer watch on our children, for better and worse.

And the creek has been rehabilitated, thanks in largest part to the Friends of Merri Creek and the Merri Creek Management Committee, established in 1988 and 1989 respectively. It's now navigable by cycling and walking paths. Factories can no longer chuck crap into the water. Most of the weeping willows have been replaced with indigenous flora, beckoning back animals not seen in a century. A few years ago we watched a yellow-tailed black cockatoo fly over – the first in my lifetime. Kookaburras and kingfishers. Echidnas. Tortoises. A month ago, near our house, a grey kangaroo. And, in recent years, the first sightings of platypuses. I have seen one myself. I came home and opened a bottle of champagne.

As "friends" of the creek, my sons have attended numerous weeding and planting days. They've seen the planning and creation of a nearby wetland, occupied now with growling grass frogs, pobblebonks and spotted marsh frogs. My youngest son collects edible weeds that grow along the Merri's banks. (Great caution required, of course: beware the poison hemlock.) He has made us wild salads and exceptional nettle gnocchi.

But this ruin and repair is the tiniest plot point in the life of the creek. English settlers abbreviated its name from the Wurundjeri-willam *merri merri* (very rocky). It was a site and source of subsistence, story and ceremony for Indigenous Australians for tens of thousands of years. The point where it joins the Yarra was used for larger tribal gatherings and historians believe the one and only land treaty, signed in 1835 between John Batman and local elders, occurred here. (Later, of course, it was indefensibly voided by the NSW governor's "terra nullius" declaration.)

These deeper, vaster wounds still require healing and reparation. Some small part of it is being quietly done here on the Merri: first and new Australians talking and toiling together, using ancient knowledge and modern resources to preserve and protect this watery vein carrying the lifeblood of Melbourne. — (M)

Three Merri birds
——
01 Sacred kingfisher
Long absent from the Creek, the kingfisher returned in 1993.
02 Tawny frogmouth
Always in pairs, they hunt in the newly revegetated area.
03 Yellow-tailed black cockatoo
Known for its distinctively raucous wail.

ABOUT THE WRITER: Myfanwy Jones is author of novels *The Rainy Season* and *LEAP* – finalist for the Miles Franklin Literary Award 2016. She also co-authored the bestselling *Parlour Games for Modern Families*.

ESSAY 03

Fighting featurism
The architecture of Robin Boyd

⎯⎯

Advocating a simple style that promoted practicality over gimmickry, Robin Boyd used his Melbourne buildings to counteract "the Australian ugliness".

by Adrian Craddock, Monocle

During a recent run, I came across a small group of people gathered on a footpath. Next to them was a sign advertising a home inspection. Normally, I wouldn't have given the scene a second thought but on this occasion I slowed down; the 20-storey building that loomed behind the pack held a great deal of interest for me. It was Domain Park Flats, the only large-scale apartment block designed by Robin Boyd (*see page 123*), arguably Australia's most revered mid-century architect.

Throughout his relatively short career (1945 to 1971), Boyd did more to democratise good design in Melbourne than any other figure. He came to prominence as the inaugural director of the Small Homes Service, an organisation that commissioned Australian architects to design cost-effective homes and then sold the blueprints to the public for a pittance. The small-footprint structures were simple enough for any qualified builder to construct, while still being comfortable, functional and sustainable. At its peak,

the service sold thousands of designs a year. Its aesthetic – all clean lines and natural materials – personified Boyd's contempt for what he called featurism, an architectural style favouring gimmicks and decoration over utility and efficiency.

"[Featurism] may be defined as the subordination of the essential whole and accentuation of selected separate features," Boyd wrote in his 1960 book *The Australian Ugliness*. "It is by no means confined to Australia or to the 20th century but it flourishes more than ever at this place and time."

"Throughout his relatively short career, Robin Boyd did more to democratise good design in Melbourne than any other figure"

Domain Park Flats represents just one of the innovative buildings Boyd designed after leaving the Small Homes Service in the early 1950s. I'd long admired the structure's restrained brick exterior, with its soaring white lift shafts exposed at the rear, but had never seen inside. I zipped up my hoody and smoothed down my hair – if I tried hard enough, perhaps the estate agent would assume I was an eccentric technology billionaire, so work-obsessed that I didn't have time to replace my frayed running shoes. The plan worked; I was directed to an apartment near the top of the tower.

The first thing that struck me was how untouched it felt. The layout demonstrated Boyd's foresight: natural light beamed through a wall of windows and low ceilings directed attention to the view. Modest bedrooms had abundant storage; the study had a drawing desk and walls flecked with oil paints. As I wondered who had left the marks, two prospective buyers entered, discussing the space. They were unsure about the proportions and would probably need to pull down the walls and start again.

I approached the balcony and stared out across the city. I could see a handful of older buildings indebted to the architectural daring Boyd fostered, including the swimming stadium constructed for the 1956 Olympics and Neil Clerehan's Fenner House. I could also make out the outline of Walsh Street, where Boyd built his own home in 1957 (*see page 113*). Perhaps the purest example of his vision for Australian modernism, it's inviting, with a form that complements its surroundings.

Looking at some of the newer residential developments nearby, I wondered what Boyd would make of how Melbourne has changed. Plenty of local architects carry the torch for his ideals – such as Clare Cousins, Charlie Inglis and John Wardle – but featurism has drifted back. Urban sprawl remains a problem and architecture has again become inaccessible to low-income earners. The result? A deluge of new homes that are inefficient, oversized and unsympathetic to nature.

Perhaps Melbourne's planners should reacquaint themselves with postwar modernism, starting with the importance of practicality in architecture. As the interior of the Domain Park Flats proves, when it comes to residential design, bigger is not always better. — (M)

Three Boyd homes
—
01 Blott House
Filled with natural light, it personifies postwar optimism.
02 Walsh Street House
Boyd's restrained residence, occasionally open to the public.
03 Featherston House
For furniture designers Grant and Mary Featherston. It has a lush indoor garden.

ABOUT THE WRITER: Adrian Craddock is MONOCLE's Melbourne correspondent. Originally from Western Australia, he is the former editor of *Smith Journal*. His favourite local café is Allpress Espresso in Collingwood.

ESSAY 04
Table talk
The city's food scene

Forget fancy. Eating out in Melbourne is like a sandwich – all the good stuff is found in the middle.

by Leanne Clancey, food writer

As a professional food writer, I'm constantly told I've got the best job in the world. However, the truth is that when you take on the role, you get three occupations in one. The first, and most obvious, is journalist. The second is forensic-level nit-picker (from which there is no time off) and the third is 24-hour on-call personal concierge to an ever-expanding platoon of hungry colleagues, cousins and former high-school friends.

It's not only recommendations for everything from clandestine date spots to vegan-friendly brunch venues that they seek. The big question posed by this unrelenting scrum is always the same: "Where's your favourite place to eat in Melbourne?"

"Here, a meal out is less a status symbol and more an accepted ritual of everyday life. We don't feel the need to punctuate occasions with flashy degustations"

It's a question I find myself ducking and weaving for two reasons: first, I want to keep my regular haunts off the radar of the masses; and second, my honest answer to the question is never as sexy as people think it should be.

And right here, dear reader, lies the humble, unadorned truth about eating out in Melbourne. Unlike high-gloss Sydney with its jaw-dropping scenery, endless sunshine and AU$50 mains, the best dining here isn't up at the pointy end – it's all found in the middle.

What we lack in landmarks and bronzed, sculpted physiques we certainly make up for in unaffected culinary sophistication and great everyday dining. Whether you seek an impeccably brewed single-origin filter coffee at 07.00, a stiff negroni at 17.00 or a midnight feast of freshly shucked Tasmanian oysters, here in Melbourne you will be consistently welcomed, respected and shown a good time.

Yes, I feel stabs of internal moral conflict about brushing off the city's (excellent) fine-dining establishments when telling people where to go but there's just something inherent to the Melburnian psyche that means we will always yearn for substance over style (even though we usually get both). In fact, this is exactly why accessible mid-range dining venues and wine bars with serious food cred have become such a staple of the city.

Melburnians love to eat out. Although the stats show we spend less per head than our friends in Sydney, we actually eat out more frequently. Here, a meal out is less a status symbol and more an accepted ritual of everyday life. We don't feel the need to punctuate special occasions with flashy, Michelin-worthy degustations (although occasionally we will). Instead, we would rather revisit a treasured "institution" or hop our way through a series of buzzy laneway venues, stopping for pre-dinner drinks at one, tapas at another and roast suckling pig at the next.

Along with its lack of pretension, another key factor that defines Melbourne's culinary scene (and you'll see it at any price point here) is a somewhat antiquated concept. One that often gets overlooked in the industry's race to keep pace with the pack and the constant need to have something new to say. It's that funny old-fashioned thing called hospitality.

For any restaurant critic, "service" is a key category used to assess a venue. Think about it though: "good service" could be little more than a friendly waiter and a plate of food that you don't have to wait too long for. Hospitality, on the other hand, the feeling of being truly looked after – well, that's something much harder to quantify and even harder to find.

The good news is that, as in Barcelona, New York and Tokyo, you can happily drink and dine solo in Melbourne and find yourself in exceptionally good hands. Better still, you don't need to pay through the nose for it. It's that knowing look, that extra piece of bread for your sauce, that perfectly timed suggestion for a Martini; it's an unspoken communication that transcends culture, language and price point.

So if you're still looking for reasons to fall in love with Melbourne then, if nothing else, let us seduce you with our smashing mid-range. — (M)

Three signs of great service
01 **Timing**
A quiet sense of urgency but unflappable composure.
02 **Sixth sense**
An uncanny ability to anticipate your needs.
03 **Warm greetings**
These speak volumes about your host.

ABOUT THE WRITER: As a Melbourne restaurant critic, food columnist and travel writer, Leanne Clancey makes plenty of reservations but had none when she signed up to be food and drink editor of our travel guide.

ESSAY 05
A massive turn-on
Graham Kennedy and Australian TV

As one of the nation's pioneering television entertainers, Graham Kennedy lifted the medium out of the 1950s and cemented Melbourne's status as a TV powerhouse.

by Ben Rylan, Monocle

Melbourne: the perfect place to make a film about the end of the world. That's how the great Hollywood actress, Ava Gardner, was reported to have described the city during production of the 1959 nuclear war drama *On the Beach*. The quote was in fact misattributed by an excitable reporter at *The Sydney Morning Herald* but that didn't stop it from etching a place in urban folklore.

The Melbourne of the 1950s probably didn't seem like a natural setting for a burgeoning cultural movement. The dreaded "six o'clock swill" – a law forcing the closure of pubs at 18.00 – was still in effect, shuffling workers in search of a post-workday tipple into the unthinkable scenario of going home to their families. Nightly news was delivered in the pages of late edition newspapers and broadcast via the airwaves of 3UZ radio. When they were on air, the city's most respected no-nonsense announcers spoke in a proper, if rather forced, faux British accent before dropping the stiff charade soon after the red "mic live" light went dim.

Then, one evening, soon after television had arrived and the 1956 Melbourne Olympics had departed, Graham Kennedy bounced onto the set of the variety show *In Melbourne Tonight*. "It's not my suit!" he warned the audience in his very own authentic Australian accent, referring to a pair of visibly too-short sleeves. "I thought I had another black one, and I haven't, and this is out of wardrobe! It could've belonged to anyone."

It was almost as if the 23-year-old had just arrived at an important dinner party only to be struck by how awkward he looked among a crowd of sophisticated grown-ups.

"Tonight, everyone is going to be doing something different," he announced during the programme's introduction, shortly after realising he'd forgotten to sit down at the desk. "I'm going to try and be good."

In Kennedy, Australians saw a larrikin, a cheeky rebel willing to derail the rules of suburban politeness for a moment's giggle before quickly setting everything back on track. His peers still marvel at how he'd always known how to be on television long before most people had worked out how to switch one on.

"Panic is like peaches and cream to me," he once said, referring to the unplanned chaos that fuelled his style. And while a punchline might sting, a key part of Kennedy's charisma was his ability to speak to his audience as all-knowing equals.

Take, for instance, any one of his many notorious advertisements, which were delivered live by the host to the camera, as was the custom then. Kennedy had spent his early years on radio broadcasting to a target audience of women of the 1950s, who would be tending to the home while their husbands worked. He knew they weren't silly enough to believe the bland scripting designed to spruik breakfast cereals, potato crisps or the unfortunately named Pussy pet food ("pussy in a can, what will they think of next?"). With a cheeky nod, Kennedy's audience was always in on the joke. It was his guests and advertisers who bore the brunt of the punchline.

If television acts as a mirror to an evolving culture then its simultaneous arrival with Kennedy helped give Australians a shared idea of who they were and the confidence to broadcast it. Issues such as feminism began a gradual ascent on the small screen when Melody Iliffe became the first female newsreader on Australian television. The industry recognised her with a Logie award in 1965 but it would be another 25 years before Melbourne's Jennifer Keyte became the first woman to anchor a commercial, prime-time, weeknight bulletin.

By the start of the 21st century, television was on the cusp of a new age. Unscripted variety no longer adhered to the amateur-style hilarity of Kennedy's anything-can-happen world. Prime-time laughs merged with social satires, including *Kath & Kim* with its riff on suburban life, and *Please Like Me*, featuring comedian Josh Thomas in a groundbreaking portrayal of a young gay man coming to grips with the confusing responsibilities of being an adult – both seminal and shot in Melbourne.

If Kennedy was to arrive on today's television screens it's hard to know how his exuberant energy and delight in breaking rules might be received amid a swell of culinary competitions and the everlasting monoculture of Australian soap operas. Then again, with a comedy genre ruled by women and a prime-time drama with

> *"In Kennedy, Australians saw a larrikin, a cheeky rebel willing to derail the rules of suburban politeness for a moment's giggle before quickly setting everything back on track"*

a gay man as the lead, maybe the young Kennedy would have been a neater fit today. While he never publicly addressed his sexuality during his lifetime, as any clued-up viewer will recall, there was never a shortage of self-referential innuendo.

The story of Melbourne's, and more broadly Australia's, evolving culture on and off the screen is filled with steps forwards, backwards and sideways. Kennedy is remembered as the man who introduced Australians to the potential of television. Maybe his famously fast wit and deep respect for the intelligence of his audience was so far ahead of its time that we're only just catching up now. — (M)

ESSAY 06

Ground rules
The cult of AFL

————

Before it was taken up nationally, the birthplace and heartland of Australian Rules football was Victoria. Today in the state capital, the sport is something of a religion.

by Andrew Mueller, Monocle

Venerable Melburnian sportswriter Martin Flanagan once described what he called "a sizeable kink" in his city's outwardly staid character: "a winter passion, which amounts to a sort of folk opera".

He was writing about football – specifically, Australian Rules. As the name suggests, it's the Australian game but it was first played in Melbourne and Melbourne remains enthralled and obsessed by it, to a degree matched by few (if any) other cities about few (if any) other sports. To visit Melbourne during football season – roughly late March to late September – without going to a match would be a preposterous dereliction.

It's not merely that Australian football itself is spectacular,

Three TV facts
————
01 Ramsay Street is real
The *Neighbours* setting is Pin Oak Court in Vermont South.
02 Richmond's Hollywood
The old Channel Nine studios were inspired by MGM.
03 The 'Please Like Me' bar
The bar seen in the opening scene is Madame Brussels in Bourke Street.

ABOUT THE WRITER: Ben Rylan is a producer at Monocle 24 and a former Melburnian who can usually be found sipping a flat white at one of London's Australian-run coffee haunts.

although it is: played on vast oval fields, a legacy of its origins as a means of keeping cricketers fit during the winter, it's swift, skilful and not infrequently brutal. It's that it's very difficult to understand Melbourne properly without knowing something of the game, so enmeshed is it with the history and mythology of the city.

The competition today known as the Australian Football League was founded in 1897 as the Victorian Football League. For most of the VFL's existence, it was a 12-club affair, with 11 teams based in Melbourne and one in Geelong, a little over an hour away by car. In the early 1980s, the League began expanding. One team, South Melbourne, was relocated to become the Sydney Swans. Another, Fitzroy, was absorbed into what is now the Brisbane Lions. Then, in 1990, the VFL rebranded as the AFL.

The Australian Football League is now a national competition (with a women's league, the AFLW, launched in 2017). Of the AFL's current roster of 18 clubs, there are two each in Queensland, New South Wales, South Australia and Western Australia. But that still leaves ten in Victoria – and nine of them in Melbourne.

These nine Melbourne clubs consist of Melbourne, North Melbourne, Richmond, Essendon, Carlton, Collingwood, Hawthorn, St Kilda and the Western Bulldogs – the latter were long known as

Footscray before an ill-advised marketing-led decision to ditch the name of the proud working-class suburb they represented. All have assiduously cultivated traditions and all are burdened by bitterly resented stereotypes.

At the upscale edge of the spectrum perches the patrician establishment club of Melbourne, which has not lowered itself to actually winning anything for several decades now. Its spiritual nemesis is Collingwood, rooted in an inner-city neighbourhood that still takes pride in an ancient reputation for ruggedness, even though the district has long since been overrun by organic coffee emporia.

"It's very difficult to understand Melbourne properly without knowing something of [AFL], so enmeshed is it with the history and mythology of the city"

Visitors attracted to ruthless conquerors may feel more at home with Hawthorn, while those with a fondness for life's thwarted underdogs will gravitate towards St Kilda. Those likely to be seduced by the melancholy of a once-imperious power coming to terms with infirmity should look at Carlton.

The rivalries between Melbourne's clubs are perhaps

less intense than they once were, when each team would play at its own ground. Following a process of rationalisation as the game was professionalised, however, almost all matches in Melbourne are now played at either the purpose-built 21st-century facility that is Docklands Stadium or the venerable cathedral of the Melbourne Cricket Ground (MCG).

The MCG provides by far the superior experience. It has occupied the same site – a short walk from downtown Melbourne – since 1853 and is now one of the world's 10 biggest sporting arenas. So with the usual exception of the football season's climactic game, the Grand Final (which fills every one of the MCG's 100,000 seats), tickets are generally available. What's more, the National Sports Museum, which is housed inside the MCG, is a brilliantly executed shrine to all of Australia's sporting obsessions.

The first-time visitor to a game need not worry – as they might at a traditional football match – about sitting in the wrong end, wearing the wrong scarf. For all that Australian football barrackers can be as rowdy as they are passionate, there is no meaningful hostility between rival supporters so crowds are not segregated by allegiance (Australian football crowds are also, to a vastly higher proportion than European football crowds, female). Fans are further united by a pantomime loathing for the game's umpires. In a delicious example of the wry deadpan that underpins the Australian humour, the AFL's officials are sponsored by OPSM – a company that manufactures spectacles. — (M)

AFL's biggest dates
——
01 Anzac Day
Collingwood play Essendon on 25 April at the MCG.
02 The Sir Doug Nicholls Indigenous Round
Named after the aboriginal footballer who played for Fitzroy.
03 Grand Final Day
The climactic clash to decide the premiership.

ABOUT THE WRITER: Andrew Mueller is a contributing editor at MONOCLE and a lifelong supporter of the Geelong Cats in the AFL. His next book will be a wilfully offbeat history of Australian Rules football.

ESSAY 07
I'm with the band
Melbourne's gigging culture

───

From no-frills pubs and
suburban backyards
to ageing band rooms, the
city's irrepressible live-
music scene continues to
endure against the odds.

by Jo Stewart,
writer

First they came for The Tote (*see
page 101*). With its sticky carpet,
graffiti-adorned toilets and
rumoured resident ghost, The
Tote is a rough-around-the-edges
pub and band room hosting punk,
metal and thrash acts on a busy
corner of Collingwood – and *the*
place to cut loose in Melbourne
since the 1980s. At least it was,
until draconian liquor licensing
regulations forced an abrupt
closure in 2010 by way
of rising security costs.

But just as the French take to
the streets to defend their 35-hour
working week, Melburnians will
give the middle finger to anyone
who dares to screw with their
music. So, carrying placards
emblazoned with slogans such
as "I Tote & I Vote", thousands of
people marched to Melbourne's
Parliament House in support of
local live-music venues at the
state's first Slam rally (Save Live
Australia's Music) that same year.
Not long after, The Tote reopened
to a collective sigh of relief.

Four years later, they came
for Cherry Bar (*see page 102*).
AC/DC Lane's iconic music venue
fell under siege thanks to noise
complaints from residents of
an apartment block that had
seemingly appeared overnight,
like the ominous spaceship in
Arrival. Once news of the crisis
spread, locals remobilised. The
venue raised AU$50,000 in 24
hours thanks to everyone from
students to industry veterans,
enough to fund soundproofing
that would allow the bar to stay
open until 05.00.

So how can Melbourne's
music scene be described to
anyone who hasn't experienced
it in all its
sweaty, beer-
soaked,
deafening
glory? While
many other
cities like to
think they're
pretty with
it, nothing
compares to
Melbourne's
depth of
talent, diversity
of genres

*"While many
other cities
like to think
they're pretty
with it, nothing
compares to
Melbourne's
depth of talent,
diversity of
genres and
commitment to
aural pleasure"*

and commitment to achieving aural pleasure.

The city is home to the newly opened Australian Music Vault, industry greats such as Molly Meldrum and artists including Camp Cope, Courtney Barnett and King Gizzard & the Lizard Wizard. Musical experiences in Melbourne range from the transcendental to the downright bizarre. You can hear lauded Canadian instrumental collective Godspeed You! Black Emperor craft an apocalyptic opus from fancy seats at the Melbourne Recital Centre and see *The Exorcist*'s Linda Blair perform a strange Halloween DJ set at Cherry Bar. You can also watch helmeted slide-guitar weirdo Bob Log III perform in an urban winery and match craft beer with classical music at an event aptly named Beerhoven.

Apart from being spoiled for choice, Melbourne's residents routinely get away with gigs that wouldn't fly elsewhere. The now defunct Applecore (an all-day, BYO festival held in a backyard in Thornbury) is a good example of pulling off a seemingly impossible gig. Like cheeky toddlers, Melburnians push boundaries to see what they can get away with. The end product is a city that has spawned some of the filthiest band names in history such as Prehistoric Douche, China Vagina, Strawberry Fist Cake, Lazertits, Tropical Fuck Storm and Amyl and the Sniffers. While the legal battles could have crushed this rabble-rousing scene forever, the near-closure of two of Melbourne's best-loved venues galvanised locals and ignited an even deeper love. It's true, you don't know what you've got until it's gone.

After the Cherry Bar fiasco, world-first laws were introduced to protect venues from noise complaints by new neighbours. This leaves locals and visitors free to spill into the nearest dingy bar, neighbourhood pub and well-trodden band room to see why Melbourne's live music scene really is the best in the world. For those about to rock, we salute you. — (M)

Three music haunts
—
01 The Curtin
Longstanding dive bar and band room.
02 Corner Hotel
A friendly pub with an impressive gig line-up.
03 The Old Bar
A Fitzroy gem with a tiny stage, misfiring pinball machine and living-room feel.

ABOUT THE WRITER: Jo Stewart is a Melbourne-based features writer, author and music aficionado. Her work has been published in *Rolling Stone*, *Vice*, *International Traveller*, *The Age*, *The Saturday Paper*, *Lonely Planet* and *Lunch Lady*.

ESSAY 08
Love thy neighbourhood
The appeal of St Kilda
———

Sure, it has a seedy side and individually its attractions may seem a little threadbare next to other suburbs, but everything about St Kilda combines to create something irresistible.

by Judith Lucy, comedian

I want to see the sun go down from St Kilda Esplanade/Where the beach needs reconstruction, where the palm trees have it hard./I'd give you all of Sydney Harbour (all that land and all that water)/For that one sweet promenade.

– From St Kilda to Kings Cross,
Paul Kelly

Frankly, I always thought those lyrics were a bit of a stretch (Sydney Harbour isn't all that bad) but having lived around that "sweet promenade" for more than 20 years, I can see what Paul Kelly is getting at. Like him, I didn't grow up in Melbourne but moved here after my first two decades in Perth. I lived in my first house share in St Kilda 25 years ago. I was a young, single comedian and the area had a fair few artists, sex workers and drug addicts – all the things my parents had warned me about – so naturally it was irresistible.

There was a faded charm to it; both the Palais Theatre *(see page 102)* and Luna Park *(see page 94)* looked older than the

entire city in which I'd grown up. The pubs weren't just places to drink and listen to cover bands but were host to comedians and singers who played original songs. The place was bursting with history, creativity and a healthy dose of danger.

The one thing that failed to impress me was the beach, probably because the Western Australian coastline where I grew up is so spectacular. Once, during a heatwave, the news showed people taking a dip at St Kilda and it looked like a Russian documentary. Melbourne is generally an indoor city – most of its inhabitants look more comfortable fully clothed in a bar than lazing by the surf. I thought, "These are my people, this is where I belong."

Because when it boils down to it, I actually love that beach with its pier and its kiosk that went up in flames in 2003 and its restaurants such as The Stokehouse, which also burnt to the ground. Both have been rebuilt and maybe that captures the area's resilience; it's changed a lot over the past 20 years but has absorbed those shifts and continues to recreate itself in a mix of the old and the new.

Fitzroy Street still has an air of decrepitude and vice, despite once having been the home to the city's finest restaurants. Café Di Stasio endures, though. My favourite waiter once told me he had to chase a woman several blocks, shouting, "Madam I believe you may have left something behind!" while clutching her underpants in some tongs. They had been left under a table. For me the story conjures up an image of St Kilda as an aging but still exotic call girl.

Cicciolina *(see page 41)* is the stalwart of Acland Street, serving fine food for more than 20 years while its cave-like back bar still welcomes artists and musicians (though they are older now and drinking

> *"Melbourne is generally an indoor city – most of its inhabitants look more comfortable fully clothed in a bar than lazing by the surf"*

top-shelf spirits). The street sadly became a backpackers' paradise long ago, with chains replacing local shops, but since becoming a street-long shopping court in recent years it too looks like it's enjoying another incarnation. However, I will always miss the original version of the Vineyard: home to some of the finest steaks and rudest service in Melbourne. I had a birthday dinner there once and my friends were told to stop singing "Happy Birthday" because the owners were trying to watch something on a television in the middle of the restaurant.

I was once going to get married in the St Kilda Botanical Gardens, which is home to a pond with my favourite sculpture, "Rain Man"; a little chap with an umbrella-fountain that rains water down on him on sunny days. That relationship didn't last and I am single again but I have many sunsets yet to watch from the Esplanade Hotel. Once, on returning from a long trip overseas, it was the first place a buddy took me. We went straight from the airport – the beer tasted fine because I knew that I was home and had Paul Kelly's song playing in my head. — (M)

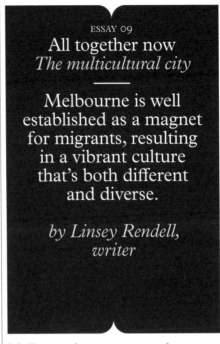

ESSAY 09
All together now
The multicultural city

——

Melbourne is well established as a magnet for migrants, resulting in a vibrant culture that's both different and diverse.

by Linsey Rendell, writer

Melbourne's present populace stems from about 200 countries and territories, speaks more than 260 languages and subscribes to 135 religious faiths. The diversity is astounding and an encouraging model for an all-inclusive utopia.

Australia has had a history of open and closed borders, plus an unhealthy dose of racism. But while this troubled past will always exist, with half of Australians born here and half born elsewhere, there is a multitude of places where social cohesion prevails.

Melbourne has always been a meeting place. To the city's Indigenous population, it's known as Naarm and encompasses the land of the Woiwurrung and Boonwurrung language groups

---

Art deco delights
—
01 Del Marie
Nautical-inspired block on
St Leonards Avenue.
02 Mandalay Flats
Admirable geometric detailing
found on The Esplanade.
03 The Royal Apartments
A mix of art deco and
modernism on Robe Street.

ABOUT THE WRITER: Judith Lucy is an award-winning Australian comedian, author and star of film and TV. Her show *Disappointments* with Denise Scott was performed at London's Soho Theatre and the Sydney Opera House.

of the greater Kulin nation. Each year (pre point of contact), these different groups would gather along the Yarra River, or Birrarung Marr, for ceremonies, celebrations and trade. From the 1940s to the 1980s, they congregated at the Builders Arms Hotel: the Fitzroy pub was an important Aboriginal Australian social and political gathering point, where Koorie, immigrants and settlers found new mates over pints of the state's bitter.

Melbourne's first camaraderie-building pubs coincided with 3,000 Chinese diggers landing in Port Phillip in time for the 1850s gold rush. Despite cultural differences and a less-than-friendly welcome, they stayed, establishing Melbourne's Chinatown, the longest ongoing Chinese settlement in the West.

The 20th century saw a new wave of Europeans, pre- and post-Second World War refugees and assisted business migrants driven to realise their full potential as shop-owners and textile manufacturers. Italians brought Australia's first pizza restaurant and installed the city's first espresso machine, while Lebanese expats rolled falafel in the north and Ethio-Eritreans dished up injera and *wat* (a type of stew) in the west. Greek, Italian and Yugoslavian arrivals were ardent believers in self-sufficiency; we have them to thank for the city's plentiful fruit trees. Today it's something of a sport to covertly forage the citrus, stonefruit and

figs that overhang the sidewalk. The fruit-lined arteries of suburbia lead to hives of cross-cultural assemblage. The beating heart of Footscray is its vibrant multicultural market. On any given day, you'll find the kind of international representation usually only seen at the UN.

In Northcote, there is a bakery called All Are Welcome.

"The arteries of suburbia lead to hives of cross-cultural assemblage... the kind of international representation usually only seen at the UN"

While its name derives from the old gold lettering that lined the front door of the former Christian Science reading room, the bakery opened during a period of awareness of the global refugee crisis and was a timely reminder of Melbourne's very open arms. Run by a Russian-born, Californian-raised immigrant, it peddles pastries reflective of the area; besides sourdough and escargots there are *ensaïmadas* (pastries from Mallorca), *medovnik* (cake from the Czech Republic) and *khachapuri* (cheesy bread from Georgia).

Down the road in Fitzroy North, the Northside Jewish Film Club gathers once a month in the underground cinema of a vintage-style bar. First and second generations from multiple cultural backgrounds come together to watch a film with Jewish people at its heart and engage in a dialogue about the themes expressed. You don't have to be Jewish to attend.

In Brunswick you can "Speed Date a Muslim". Created by Muslim feminist Hana Assafiri of the Moroccan Soup Bar (*see page 34*), the weekly event sees Muslim women and non-Muslims gather to ask any (respectful) questions they like about Islam. With more than 100,000 Muslims from 60 countries living in the city, it's an important era for debunking Islamophobia.

Living in a culturally diverse society has its complexities but Melbourne has embraced an inclusive character and fostered an empathetic people, passionate about change. Here I can be a student of the world, without needing to leave my inner-suburban bubble. — (M)

Meals with meaning
—
01 Tamil Feasts
Moreish Tamil cooking by Tamil men.
02 Scarf
Pop-up dinners providing training for migrant communities.
03 Long Street Coffee
Employs young people from refugee backgrounds.

ABOUT THE WRITER: Linsey Rendell is a writer and photographer in a constant state of unrest. When she's not producing travel stories, she scribbles about equality, the environment and social change.

ESSAY 10
Screen queen
Movie-going in Melbourne
—
From the first narrative feature-length film to the first US-style drive-in, Melbourne has a rich cinematic history. And Melburnians will never tire of telling you all about it.

by Tara Judah, film critic

I first fell in love at 15, when I stepped inside the grand foyer at Melbourne's Astor Theatre (*see page 103*). As the gold curtains opened and the lights went down, I fell deeper. Two hours later, when the lights came up, I saw the soon-to-be-standard chocolate stains on my jeans. All Melburnians will be familiar with this stain, an unavoidable consequence of having enjoyed a handmade choc-top (an ice-cream cone dipped in chocolate) at the cinema. This experience would become a weekly ritual in my teenage years and set me up for a lifetime of falling in love, over and over again, with Melbourne cinemas.

Australians love to spin a yarn and we'll tell anyone who will listen that we made the world's first ever narrative feature-length film. But as a Melburnian, I also get to boast that we were the first city to screen it. The Lumière Brothers held the first public film screening in the world in 1895 and by October 1896 ye olde Melburnians were taking up their seats at the Athenaeum (*see page 104*), in the very heart of the city on

Collins Street. A decade later, the first full-length feature – which was also filmed in and around the city – had its first screening. It was 1906 and it was a true-blue tall Aussie tale, *The Story of the Kelly Gang.*

In the following years cinemas opened like wildfire. Fewer grand picture palaces were built in the years between the two World Wars but many withstood the challenges. In the postwar period, entertainment in the city flourished once more. The government's rallying cry of "Populate or perish" brought Brits and Europeans to Melbourne in the millions.

By the 1950s Melbourne could consider itself a global cinema city. In 1952, six years after Cannes, Melbourne got its first film festival. The Melbourne International Film Festival (MIFF) is now one of the longest-running film festivals in the world. In 1954 the suburb of Burwood hosted the first Australian version of a US-style drive-in.

> "Australians love to spin a yarn and we'll tell anyone who will listen that we made the world's first narrative feature-length film"

But then, in 1956, the Olympic Games came to town and every home wanted its own television set. The great cinema decline continued into the 1960s and 1970s, with many majestic theatres being demolished, twinned or multiplexed.

Happily, 12 independent cinemas across the city survived, thanks to a Greek cinema and theatre chain. The Greek community in Melbourne had led to a demand for Greek-language entertainment, including weekly newsreels from home.

Trouble hit again in the 1980s, with the arrival of multilingual television station SBS and the shiny new technology: VHS. Among the casualties was one of my favourites: the famous fleapit Lumiere on Lonsdale Street, where I saw many risqué French films (always making sure to put my coat down on the seat before sitting. I also have fond memories of my first ushering job at Kino on Collins. Across the city, you can still get a glimpse of the past. There's the Rivoli in Camberwell and the Westgarth in Northcote, the Sun in Yarraville (*see page 104*) and Carlton's Cinema Nova, where "best choc-top" wars play out. And I bet you can still find grains of rice in between the seats at the Astor – something audiences threw when Ralph and Betty got married in *The Rocky Horror Picture Show*.

Today the Melbourne cinema scene has expanded to include outdoor and pop-up ventures such as Rooftop on Swanston Street (*see page 104*). For the serious cinephile there's the Cinémathèque at ACMI and Melbourne has the biggest IMAX theatre in the world (thanks to the closure of the one in Sydney). So wherever you take up a seat in the dark, the city's tall stories and its rich history are sure to melt your heart. Or, at least, melt the top of your choc-top, leaving you with a little memento of Melbourne cinema. — (M)

Three picture palaces
———

01 The Astor Theatre, St Kilda
Old-school double-features.
02 Forum Theatre, CBD
The palatial decor creates a real sense of occasion.
03 Capitol Theatre, CBD
Extraordinary geometric plaster ceiling.

ABOUT THE WRITER: Tara Judah is a film critic, programmer and broadcaster. She managed the programming for Melbourne's iconic Astor Theatre and regularly dissects film on the airwaves, including at Triple R and Monocle 24.

Culture
—— Broaden
your mind

Museums
Exhibiting attention

Melbourne's informal
moniker of "Australia's
cultural capital" may
have been born out of a
long-standing rivalry with
Sydney but the reality
is that decades have
been spent nurturing
cultural output to earn the
title. And while much of
Melbourne's reputation
may rest on excellent food,
coffee and wine, its artistic
pedigree commands just
as much attention.

Internationally revered
institutions and carefully
curated curiosities rub
shoulders with a standout
selection of performance
venues, a dynamic
street-art movement and
a lively arts offering, not
to mention a remarkably
resilient independent
cinema scene. The story
of Melbourne's cultural
clout has been a long time
in the making. Now it's
ready for its close-up.

①
Heide Museum of Modern
Art, Bulleen
Cultural trove

In the outer suburb of Bulleen
is a grassy plot that was bought
by John and Sunday Reed in
1934. Right up to their deaths
(10 days apart) in 1981, they
worked to enrich Australia's
cultural offering, housing
artists such as Sidney Nolan,
Joy Hester and Albert Tucker.

Later the couple sold the
property and contents to the
Victorian government to be
used as a public art museum.
The top-notch collection
makes it well worth tackling
the tricky transport to get here.
*7 Templestowe Road, 3105
+61 (0)3 9850 1500
heide.com.au*

3

Old Treasury Building,
East Melbourne
Urban evolution

Designed by the talented
architect JJ Clark in the 1850s
(*see page 112*), Melbourne's
Old Treasury became "old"
within about 20 years of its
unveiling, when the treasury
offices were relocated. Today
it's a museum with exhibitions
detailing the evolution of the
city's skyline, the role of the
gold rush in its urban growth
and how six self-governing
colonies became the nation
of Australia, with Melbourne
its first national capital. It also
features visiting exhibitions that
recount the many tales which
have made this modern city.
20 Spring Street, 3000
+61 (0)3 9651 2233
oldtreasurybuilding.org.au

2

Old Melbourne Gaol, CBD
Lock it in

Every Australian knows the
story of Ned Kelly. The days
of bushrangers terrorising
rural communities are said to
have ended after the shootout
between police and the Kelly
Gang in Glenrowan but Kelly's
influence on Australian culture
has never faded.

The complexities of the
folk hero are perhaps best
explored here, at the scene of
his hanging on 11 November
1880. Just a short walk away
at the State Library, you'll find
his bullet-riddled armour worn
in that fateful final gunfight.
377 Russell Street, 3000
+61 (0)3 9656 9889
oldmelbournegaol.com.au

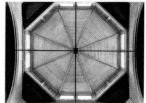

④ The ANZ Banking Museum, CBD
Wealth of knowledge

The evolution of currency may not leap out as a winning concept for a museum but consider this: in the early years of Australia's British settlements, there was no currency at all. Transactions were performed using valuables as varied as rum and bundles of wheat. Unsurprisingly, it was chaos until colonies and corporations introduced coins and tokens.

On the lower-ground floor of the Gothic Bank building on Collins Street, this museum traces the evolution of trade from Indigenous communities and early coin designs (including the "holey dollar", a repurposed Spanish coin) to today's polymer banknotes. The museum also features a collection of classic uniforms.
380 Collins Street, 3000
+61 (0)3 8655 5152

I didn't think this through...

⑤ Screen Worlds (ACMI), CBD
Watch and learn

Television may have arrived a little late in Australia (just in time for the 1956 Melbourne Olympics) but its rich, small-screen history is brilliantly captured at this museum offshoot of the Australian Centre for the Moving Image. Explore the international success of *Skippy the Bush Kangaroo*, the cultural place occupied by soaps such as *Neighbours* and the early series *Homicide*, with its continuing influence on Australia's appetite for gritty crime stories.
Federation Square, Flinders Street, 3000
+61 (0)3 8663 2200
acmi.net.au

Arts companies

01 **Victorian Opera:** Where else might you find Watkin Wombat from *The Magic Pudding*, mixing with Rossini's *William Tell*? Its blend of classics, modern interpretations and new works makes this one of Australia's leading arts institutions.
victorianopera.com.au

02 **The Production Company:** This local firm brings international musical theatre to Melbourne. Past hits have included *The Boy from Oz* and *Mame*, starring theatre icon Rhonda Burchmore.
theproductioncompany. com.au

03 **Melbourne Theatre Company:** Since 1953 the MTC has promoted Australian storytelling on stage with annual seasons of plays, regular festivals and initiatives aimed at encouraging creativity.
mtc.com.au

04 **The Australian Conservatoire of Ballet:** This training institution has polished the pirouettes of some of the world's leading dancers. It also hosts fine ballet productions.
acbaustralia.com.au

Properties we trust
——
In 1938, Canadian silent-film actress Claire Adams moved to Melbourne with her Australian husband. Their country estate, Mooramong, is perfectly preserved by the National Trust and one of many notable locations often open to visitors.
nationaltrust.org.au

6
Melbourne Museum, Carlton
Tales of the city

From social and Indigenous
history to science and the
environment, this ambitious
museum aims to showcase all
that has made Melbourne what
it is – from prehistory to the
present. Museums with such a
wide mandate risk overloading
visitors with information but all
the attractions here are rooted
in the story of the city, be it
the enormous skeleton of a
Mamenchisaurus or the tale of
Phar Lap, a racehorse whose
winning streak and mysterious
demise still generate chatter at
the annual Melbourne Cup.
11 Nicholson Street, 3053
+61 (0)3 8341 7777
museumsvictoria.com.au

Park life
———
Of the many amusement
parks around the world
carrying the Luna name, Luna
Park in St Kilda, open since
1912, is the oldest in operation.
Its careful preservation
and enviable location
make it a quintessential
Melbourne locale.
lunapark.com.au

Day trips
Enriching excursions

**01 — 03 Bendigo Art Gallery,
Bendigo:** Given the plentiful
offerings of world-class
cultural institutions within
Melbourne, it may come as
a surprise to discover that
one of Australia's finest
galleries is located two hours
outside the city in the gold
rush-era town of Bendigo.
Past attractions have included
exhibitions dedicated to
Finnish design brand
Marimekko and legendary
costume designer Edith Head,
as well as a revealing look
at the 350-year history of
fashionable underwear.
bendigoartgallery.com.au

**04 Castlemaine Art
Museum, Castlemaine:**
This impressive museum
is housed inside a beautiful
1930s art deco building and
was nearly forced to close in
2017 before an anonymous
11th-hour donation secured
its future for the next two
years. With cafés serving
tasty produce from around
the area, and a thriving old
picture palace, a train ride
to Castlemaine makes for
a pleasant day out.
castlemainegallery.com

01

02

03

04

(1)
National Gallery of
Victoria, Southbank
National treasure

Melbourne hasn't been
Australia's official political
capital since the late 1920s but
to the city's proud citizens it's
still the cultural one. It's of little
surprise, then, that the National
Gallery of Victoria is the
country's most visited gallery.

The entrance on St Kilda
Road resembles one you might
imagine belonging to a fortress
in a modern Grimms' fairytale;
with its fountains and water
walls, the NGV is as noted for its
architecture by Roy Grounds
as for its collection. The home
of Melbourne's design week,
world-class architecture and
fashion events, as well as the
city's Triennial, it's an attraction
on an international scale.
180 St Kilda Road, 3006
+61 (0)3 8620 2222
ngv.vic.gov.au

3

Centre for Contemporary Photography, Fitzroy
Exposing pictures

A bright white box on the corner of George and Kerr streets in Fitzroy, the Centre for Contemporary Photography (CCP) was established in 1986 as a not-for-profit shared resource centre. The space may be petite but the calendar of exhibitions, workshops and events has played an integral role over the past few decades in defining the city's photographic offering. "CCP adds great value to the visual culture of Melbourne," says director Naomi Cass.
404 George Street, 3065
+61 (0)3 9417 1549
ccp.org.au

2

Australian Centre for Contemporary Art, Southbank
Leading the cultural charge

Fittingly, one of the country's leading collections of contemporary art is housed inside an award-winning architectural sensation by Melbourne-based Roger Wood and Randal Marsh in the city's Southbank arts precinct. Created in 1983 and housed here since 2002, ACCA has played a leading role in keeping Melbourne on the cultural map. With its eclectic mix of international exhibitions and locally focused fare, the ACCA is an unmissable stop-off.
111 Sturt Street, 3006
+61 (0)3 9697 9999
acca.melbourne

4

Ian Potter Centre, CBD
All Australian, all exceptional

The NGV's younger sibling occupies a generous space on Federation Square, just across the Yarra. It also carries the impressive distinction of being the first major gallery in the world to focus exclusively on Australian art.

A visit here is like a walking tour through the nation's history, from Aboriginal and Torres Strait Islander art to pieces from the Colonial era and the contemporary works defining Australia's cultural landscape today. The space is divided into numerous galleries and offers a tidy collection of prints, photography, fashion, textiles and decorative arts.
Federation Square, Russell Street, 3000
+61 (0)3 8620 2222
ngv.vic.gov.au

5

Gertrude Contemporary, Preston
Look to the future

The unwavering aim at Gertrude Contemporary is to keep an artistic eye on the young voices of tomorrow. And while that may seem like a fairly common objective, the public gallery is following through: few artists who have represented Australia at the Venice Biennale in recent decades can look back on their careers without paying tribute to Gertrude.

Named after its first location in a former textile factory in inner-city Fitzroy, the centre has since relocated to an impressive modern space in the city's north.
21-31 High Street, 3072
+61 (0)3 9419 3406
gertrude.org.au

6

Abbotsford Convent, Abbotsford
Art worshippers

Eleven buildings across more than six hectares make up this delightful former monastic site, now a first-rate arts hub. The convent is run by a non-profit organisation and houses more than 100 artistic studios, two galleries, a cosy café and a radio station dedicated to fine local talent.

This hive of artistic activity is even more abuzz in the warmer months, when picnickers flock to the lush gardens. It's not often that such a historic space winds up in the hands of a group of art enthusiasts.
1 Saint Heliers Street, 3067
+61 (0)3 9415 3600
abbotsfordconvent.com.au

Commercial galleries
Where to buy

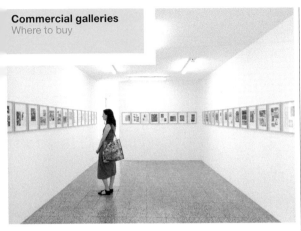

1

Neon Parc, CBD
Low-key, high quality

An unofficial rule governs
how Melburnians judge a
venue's "Melbourne-ness",
whether it be a café, bar, or
gallery: if it's small and poky,
hidden down a labyrinth of
lanes and free from obvious
signage, it's sure to be a hit
with the city's creative folk.

This petite gallery ticks
all the boxes and has been
delighting contemporary-art
lovers since 2006 with works
by Dale Frank, Rob McLeish,
and Elizabeth Pulie among its
enviable line-up. The gallery
also operates an outpost
in the artistically inclined
neighbourhood of Brunswick,
just a short tram ride away
in the north of the city. Open
from Wednesday to Saturday.
1/53 Bourke Street, 3000
+61 (0)3 9663 0911
neonparc.com.au

2

Daine Singer, CBD
New and exciting

Though it's less than 10 years
old, this gallery in Melbourne's
city centre is anything but a
junior player on the commercial
scene. Just 15 artists from
across Australia and New
Zealand are represented here,
ensuring the offering is always
finely crafted, well tuned and
on point.
*Basement, 325 Flinders
Lane, 3000*
+61 (0)410 264 036
dainesinger.com

3

Anna Schwartz Gallery, CBD
Central and vibrant

This gallery has been a mainstay
of the Melbourne art scene
since opening in 1986 and
boasts a coveted location in a
historic building on Flinders
Lane, near some of the city's
finest bars and restaurants. It
represents both established
and emerging artists – mostly
Australian – including the
fantastical and candid Brisbane
painter Jenny Watson and
Melbourne-based sculptor
Emily Floyd. The gallery's
continued relevance is a
testament to the city centre's
vibrant arts scene.
185 Flinders Lane, 3000
+61 (0)3 9654 6131
annaschwartzgallery.com

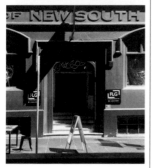

④

Flinders Lane Gallery, CBD
Moving with the times

Housed behind the dark
façade of the old Bank of New
South Wales and surrounded
by some of the city's most
visited lanes, this gallery was
one of the forces that helped
refresh Melbourne's art scene
throughout the 1990s.

The city's artistic output has
ballooned in the years since,
with rival galleries popping
up in every direction. Flinders
Lane Gallery has evolved with
the city while retaining its
status as a hub for multifaceted
contemporary art.
137 Flinders Lane, 3000
+61 (0)3 9654 3332
flg.com.au

⑤

Original & Authentic
Aboriginal Art, CBD
Indigenous pieces

Not so long ago, dodgy salesmen
had a monopoly on Indigenous
art for sale. Today it's much
easier to find contemporary,
ethically sourced works.

Focusing on the Central and
Western deserts, Arnhem Land
and the Kimberley, founding
director Alexis Hessen's gallery
is one of Melbourne's better
destinations for Aboriginal
art. It represents prominent
talents such as Goody Barrett,
Margaret Scobie and Walala
Tjapaltjarri. It's also a member
of the City of Melbourne's
Indigenous Code of Conduct,
which ensures authenticity and
the ethical treatment of artists.
90 Bourke Street, 3000
+61 (0)3 9663 5133
*originalandauthenticaboriginal
art.com*

Laneway galleries

01 **Hosier Lane, CBD:**
This small bluestone
lane's artistic reputation
gained prominence in the
1990s before peaking in
2010 when the city council
unwisely ordered a Banksy
to be painted over. Today
only sightseers disturb
the artists at work.

02 **Rutledge Lane, CBD:**
Artist Adrian Doyle
ignited a mixed reaction
when he erased the
work of all those before
him by covering this
entire backstreet next to
Hosier Lane in a shade
of icy blue. When it
comes to Melbourne's
street art, nothing stays
the same for long.

03 **AC/DC Lane, CBD:**
Since 2004 this popular
lane has been the city's
tribute to the legendary
band from which it takes
its name. Fittingly, it's also
home to one of the city's
favourite rock music
nightspots, Cherry Bar
(*see page 102*).

The Tote, Collingwood
Rock of ages

Melbourne's self-proclaimed "home of rock" can be found inside a classic old corner pub and has provided a stage for the city's thriving local music scene for decades. But it wasn't so long ago that its days seemed numbered.

A dispute over the cost of liquor licensing forced The Tote's closure in 2010, a move that was quickly reversed by the local government when thousands of protesters emerged demanding the venue remain open. Fortunately for Collingwood's nightlife, the bar's continued survival still attracts crowds in search of good music and, in some cases, the resident ghost.
71 Johnston Street, 3066
+61 (0)3 9419 5320
thetotehotel.com

Live venues
Performance spaces

1
Malthouse Theatre, Southbank
Acting cool

Since its inception in 1976, this group has been known as the Hoopla Theatre Foundation and the Playbox Theatre Company. Today, as Malthouse Theatre, it's one of the country's pre-eminent performance companies.

A multidisciplinary approach to Australian material has won praise from critics around the world and its 2009 production of *Exit the King*, adapted by Geoffrey Rush and Neil Armfield, was restaged on Broadway. Now performing out of Southbank's former Coopers brewery and malthouse (hence its most recent name), this company should be top of the list for those interested in contemporary theatre.
113 Sturt Street, 3006
+61 (0)3 9685 5111
malthousetheatre.com.au

Five more live venues

01 The Forum, CBD:
Designed by architect
John Eberson, who
cultivated the concept
of atmospheric theatres,
this grand old palace is
perennially popular.
forummelbourne.com.au

02 Cherry Bar, CBD:
Founded by the former
drummer of punk-rock
band Cosmic Psychos,
this laneway bar carries
a lot of street cred.
cherrybar.com.au

**03 Melbourne Recital
Centre, Southbank:**
This striking twin
auditorium has hosted
some of the city's finest
musical performances
since 2009.
melbournerecital.com.au

**04 Sidney Myer Music
Bowl, South Yarra:**
This favourite outdoor
performance space (*see
page 113*) was inspired
by the famous Hollywood
Bowl in Los Angeles.
*artscentremelbourne.
com.au*

**05 Chapel Off Chapel,
Prahran:** A former
church, this space
was reborn in 1995
as a unique venue for
intimate performances
chapeloffchapel.com.au

3
Palais Theatre, St Kilda
The beat goes on

One of Melbourne's finest music venues started out as a picture palace in 1927; its original owners also created Luna Park (*see page 139*), one of the world's few remaining amusement parks from the early 1900s.

Despite attracting performers such as the Rolling Stones, Roy Orbison and Alanis Morissette, it was stuck in a perpetual state of pending closure. But after a AU$26m refurbishment in 2017, the Palais' status as a leading lady has been restored.
*Corner of Lower Esplanade
and Cavell streets, 3182
+61 (0)3 8537 7677
palaistheatre.com.au*

4
The Wheeler Centre, CBD
All talk

Take the Speakers' Corner concept from London's Hyde Park, mix it with a dash of Melbourne's cultural sophistication and add a dose of Australia's freshest thinkers and you'll get something like The Wheeler Centre. This lively hive of chatter adjoining the State Library opened in 2008 when Melbourne became a Unesco City of Literature. With a colourful programme of debates, presentations and talks, there's no better place to have a conversation – or just listen to one.
*176 Little Lonsdale Street, 3000
+61 (0)3 9094 7809*

Just try and stop us!

Cinemas
Screen doors

①

The Astor Theatre, St Kilda
Big-screen drama

The fondness Melburnians share for the treasured Astor Theatre plays like any epic love story of the silver screen. The classic picture palace opened in 1936 and, while many other cinemas faded away during the 1970s and 1980s, it survived by screening Greek-language films for the city's growing community before reverting to its now famous repertory double-bill format.

When the cinema was threatened with closure in 2012 and 2014 (a common story here), loyal patrons rushed to its defence, signing petitions and enlisting local media. Their efforts paid off: today, the Astor is one of the most talked-about jewels in Melbourne's cultural crown with state-of-the-art digital projectors, 35mm and 70mm film screenings, a popular bar and even a resident cat called Duke. The theatre's charming calendar posters also make great souvenirs.
*Corner of Chapel Street and Dandenong Road, 3182
+61 (0)3 9510 1414
astortheatre.net.au*

②
Lido Cinemas, Hawthorn
More than just films

Melburnians are a sophisticated bunch and that's rarely more evident than on Friday evenings at Hawthorn's Lido cinema. The leafy neighbourhood has long carried a reputation as a somewhat awkward blend of old manors and scruffy university crowds but the Lido is helping to give it a fresh look.

With an informed selection of world cinema, a rooftop screening area and a dedicated jazz room, this is one of Melbourne's finest cultural destinations.
675 Glenferrie Road, 3122
+61 (0)3 8658 0000
lidocinemas.com.au

③
Rooftop, CBD
High life

Ascend to the seventh floor of Swanston Street's Curtin House during the day and you may not notice the cinema screen at one end of the rooftop. Much of this venue's life is spent as a bar with panoramic views but by night it screens an expertly chosen mix of cult classics and new releases.

The arrival of Rooftop in 2003 set off a race among the city's other elevated business owners to introduce their own sky-diners but this one has extra charm. Look out for the local beers on tap.
252 Swanston Street, 3000
+61 (0)3 9654 5394
rooftopcinema.com.au

First in line

The first film to screen in Australia was shown at the Athenaeum in 1896. Ten years later, the venue hosted the premiere of the film that many consider to be the world's first dramatic feature, *The Story of the Kelly Gang*.
athenaeumclub.com.au

④
Sun Theatre, Yarraville
Shining example

For years Melbourne's west was derided as the sleepy home of the city's old working-class suburbs but no longer: Footscray, Seddon and Yarraville now feature popular bars, cafés, shops and sought-after properties.

Given the rapid urban transformation here, the presence of the Sun Theatre is a welcome surprise. The art deco cinema opened as a single-screen auditorium in 1938 but has since been respectfully split into eight boutique screening rooms. Highlights include small tables between seats, the iconic neon sign and a standout selection of choc-tops (Australia's age-old cinema ice-cream treat).
8 Ballarat Street, 3013
+61 (0)3 9362 0999
suntheatre.com.au

Choc-top, popcorn, choc-top...

Melbourne on screen

01 Animal Kingdom (2010):
Ever since the Australian television series *Homicide* made Melbourne the backdrop to its gritty tales, the city has had a noir-like allure for storytellers. This brilliant crime drama from writer and director David Michôd was inspired by true events and landed local veteran actor Jacki Weaver an Oscar nomination.

02 Head On (1998):
This adaptation of the first novel by Melbourne author Christos Tsiolkas sees a young gay man (Alex Dimitriades) from a conservative Greek family in a nightmarish after-dark vision of Melbourne. Directed by Ana Kokkinos, it's part social realism, part art-drama.

03 Picnic at Hanging Rock (1975): Director Peter Weir's adaptation of Joan Lindsay's novel may be Australia's most celebrated film. Its eerie ambiguity about the fate of a group of schoolgirls on Valentine's Day in 1900 continues to draw visitors to Hanging Rock outside Melbourne. Rarely is an unsettling mystery given such subtle beauty.

Tick of approval

To keep track of the city's restaurant openings, snappiest shops and unmissable events, Melburnians turn to online resource *Broadsheet*. Founded in Melbourne by Nick Shelton in 2009, this now nationwide resource has its finger permanently on the pulse.
broadsheet.com.au

Media round-up
Mag raves and airwaves

1
Media
Read all about it

Melbourne's print publications are thriving. **❶** *Frankie* appeals to young Australian creatives while **❷** *Smith Journal*, its quarterly little brother, has a masculine bent. When it comes to newspapers, **❸** *The Age* has been informing the city since 1854 and is joined today by **❹** *The Saturday Paper*, which offers longform journalism and careful analysis. **❺** *The Monthly*, from the folk behind *The Saturday Paper*, is a political journal in the mould of *The New Yorker*. **❻** *The Lifted Brow* offers commentary, criticism, fiction and poetry, while **❼** *Green* is a design and architecture magazine with a loyal readership. Last but not least, **❽** *Treadlie* caters to the city's discerning pedal-pushers and **❾** *Offscreen* is beloved by technology enthusiasts.

Radio

01 ABC 774 (774 AM):
A local station operated by Australia's public broadcaster (ABC), with a focus on news and current affairs.

02 JOY 94.9 (94.9 FM):
Australia's first radio station dedicated to the queer community and staffed almost entirely by volunteers.

03 Triple R (102.7 FM):
Helping Melbourne's homegrown music scene to thrive, Triple R's hosts maintain total control over their musical offering.

04 Kiss FM (87.6 and 87.8 FM): Created by dance music enthusiasts in the 1990s as an antidote to what was then a glut of rock on other stations.

Design and architecture
—— The built environment

Thanks to a flush of cash courtesy of the 19th-century gold rush, Melbourne's urban core is dotted with picturesque brick terraces, grand public buildings and more iron lacework than any other city on Earth. For such a young country, this noticeable mark of Victorian-era heritage is unique. However, beyond this immediate built identity lies a selection of brutalist and modernist structures that are the real quiet achievers.

In the mid to late 20th century, influential Australian architects such as Robin Boyd and Peter McIntyre forged their careers in Melbourne and developed a school of thought based on innovative techniques and styles better suited to the local climes. This unabashed ingenuity has not only informed subsequent generations of impressive contemporary architects but also created a receptive public and government following. Read on to uncover our pick of the finest buildings from each of these eras.

Gold rush era
National treasures

①
Royal Exhibition
Building, Carlton
Show and tell

As the industrial revolution
brought about a frenzy of new
inventions such as typewriters,
lawnmowers and electric
lights, international exhibitions
began popping up to show
off these advancements. Keen
for the world to admire its
gold rush-fuelled clout,
Melbourne set about building
a monumental hall to host
the 1880 to 1881 Melbourne
International Exhibition.

Joseph Reed designed the
main brick hall, which is what
remains today. The interiors
have undergone several facelifts
but between 1990 and 1994
John Ross Anderson's ornate
pastel decorative scheme
from 1901 (designed for the
opening of Federal Parliament,
no less) was reinstated. Now
heritage-listed, Melbourne's
Royal Exhibition Building is
the world's only surviving 19th-
century "Palace of Industry"
that remains on its original
site. Tours can be organised
through the Melbourne
Museum (*see page 94*).
9 Nicholson Street, 3053
+61 (0)3 9270 5000
museumsvictoria.com.au

②
State Library Victoria, CBD
Roman holiday

The State Library was Joseph
Reed's first foray into civic
architecture. He won an
architectural competition to
design the library with his
Roman revival-style plans and
construction began in 1854.
While the first phase of the
central vestibule was completed
in 1856, development
continued in various stages: for
example in 1961 the northwest
pavilion was added, followed by
the La Trobe Library in 1965.
All successive architects drew
on Reed's original plans.

The iconic Reading Room,
with its impressive dome
measuring 34.75 metres in
diameter, was added in 1913
and is said to be inspired by
the US Library of Congress.
328 Swanston Street, 3000
+61 (0)3 8664 7000
slv.vic.gov.au

Victorian-era houses
Home front

Heritage housing

Before the advent of fiercely
Australian-led design in the
1950s, Melbourne homes were
based on European templates.
When money was rolling in
from the gold rush, developers
borrowed and adapted British
architectural styles.

As a result, many inner-
city neighbourhoods such as
Fitzroy and Brunswick are
packed with rows of double-
story Victorian terraces. Mainly
built from brick, and sometimes
native bluestone, these houses
feature ornate details such as
stucco and timber balconies
on the outside and stained-
glass windows, polished floors
and intricate architraves and
cornices within.

Meanwhile, the western
suburbs of Seddon and
Yarraville were traditionally
working-class neighbourhoods
and therefore retain smaller,
single-fronted cottages with
pitched, corrugated-iron roofs.
More affordable materials such
as timber and weatherboard
define the aesthetic but, like
all houses from this era,
there's a heavy-handed swirl
of decorative iron lacework.
Once pegged as affordable
options by which to climb
onto the property ladder,
these heritage homes became
popular investments in the
mid-1990s. Freshly renovated
versions sold for exorbitant
amounts, driving the price tag
of their yet-to-be-restored
neighbours sky high.

Art deco
Ornate achievements

Sun Theatre, Yarraville
Visual delights

Built in 1938 with a AU$44,500 price tag, the cheery Sun Theatre was designed by the Cowper, Murphy and Appleford firm and featured a single, 1,050-seat auditorium decked out with lavish trimmings. After running as a Greek-language cinema, the complex closed in 1982 and sat neglected until the current owners purchased the property in 1995.

It took two and a half years and AU$350,000 to restore the crumbling cinema to its art deco glory. The large auditorium was divided into four smaller screening rooms and in 2002 further work saw the addition of four more screens, with the owners using silicon moulds to replicate the original plaster work.
8 Ballarat Street, 3013
+61 (0)3 9362 0999
suntheatre.com.au

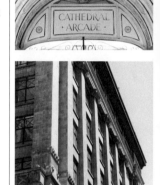

Nicholas Building, CBD
One of many

Harry Norris populated the city skyline with the Majorca Building, Mitchell House, Curtin House and the Nicholas Building, leaving perhaps the most fingerprints on Melbourne's commercial art deco offering.

It's said that Norris, who looked to the US for inspiration, followed the commercially minded principles of the Chicago School style of architecture: using a steel frame flanked by masonry exteriors, he built high to maximise office space. The 1926 Nicholas Building is probably his most celebrated art deco work and retains the original Doric columns at its base, towering pilasters above and an arcade canopied by stained glass and leadlight arches.
37 Swanston Street, 3000
nicholasbuilding.org.au

3

Manchester Unity
Building, CBD
Ahead of its time

This neo-gothic office block
was erected in just eight
months in 1932. Melbourne
architect Marcus Barlow
fulfilled his brief to design a
building with "every modern
convenience", including the
city's first escalator (used by
60,000 people on its first day)
and three passenger lifts.

The exteriors are coated
with glazed terracotta tiles and
the interiors decorated with
mosaics and sandblasted black
marble. Dental practitioner
Dr Kia Pajouhesh now owns
a substantial portion of the
building and has restored many
original features, including the
boardroom on Level 11, with
its six-metre-long table topped
by a single glass plate.
220 Collins Street, 3000
manchesterunitybuilding.com.au

Modernist
Postwar projects

1

Heide II, Bulleen
One with nature

This postwar residence,
built for art patrons John and
Sunday Reed, won the Victorian
Enduring Architecture Prize in
2016. When briefing architects
David McGlashan and Neil
Everist in 1964, the couple
requested a home that was
"a gallery to be lived in" and
whose considered modernist
form would weather and blend
into the surrounding property.

Tucked beneath native
gum trees on a Yarra flood
plain, the exteriors of
oxidised iron beams, timber,
glass and Mount Gambier
limestone besser blocks
nestle harmoniously into the
landscape. Inside, the dappled
Australian sunlight filters
through to the simple and cosy
living spaces that now house
rotating exhibitions for the
Heide Museum of Modern
Art (*see page 91*). Between the
house and its sculpture park
there's also a kitchen garden
growing herbs, vegetables and
roses, planted by Sunday in the
mid-1960s and modelled on
that of an English cottage.
*7 Templestowe Road, 3105
+61 (0)3 9850 1500
heide.com.au*

2

1 Treasury Place,
East Melbourne
Good neighbours

At the tender age of 19,
architect JJ Clark drafted the
plans for what is now known
as the Old Treasury Building.
Constructed between 1858
and 1862, it was eventually
heralded as one of the
country's best-executed
renaissance-revival structures.

Today, Clark's heavy-handed
application of ornamentation
on the blocked sandstone
façade sits in stark contrast
with the adjacent 1960s
International-style office
building of 1 Treasury Place.
The government requested
that Barry Patten of Yuncken
Freeman match the new
building's proportions and
scale to that of its historic
neighbour. The result is
an impressive feat that sees
the precast concrete grid of
1 Treasury Place marrying
seamlessly with its more
mature companion.
1 Treasury Place, 3002

Down by the river

The cantilevered triangular
home of late modernist architect
Peter McIntyre (*see page 123*)
sits on the banks of the Yarra
in Kew, alongside several
outbuildings and studios.
McIntyre River Residence
isn't open to the public, so
the best chance of a glimpse
is from the river.

❸

Sidney Myer Music Bowl, South Yarra
Music for the masses

South of the Yarra in the Kings Domain Gardens stands a spindly tensile canopy built from plywood and sheets of aluminium secured by a network of steel cables. Beneath this taut awning sits a stage and before it is a swell of grass for seating.

The postwar freeform Sidney Myer Music Bowl was opened in 1959 and designed by Barry Patten, who drew inspiration from the Hollywood Bowl in Los Angeles. The Myer Foundation – named for the late department store founder, music-lover and philanthropist Sidney Myer – built it as a democratic music venue for the people of Melbourne and it continues to host free, open-air concerts by the Melbourne Symphony Orchestra and ticketed international headliners.
Kings Domain Gardens, Linlithgow Avenue, 3000
artscentremelbourne.com.au

What a charming canopy

❹

Robin Boyd Foundation, South Yarra
Driving Australian design

Architect, educator, writer and critic Robin Boyd (*see page 123*) was one of modern Australia's most influential urbanist voices. Rising to prominence in the 1950s and 1960s, he was a formidable force behind the establishment of a national architectural identity.

From his Walsh Street home to 200-plus housing blocks, each of his projects considered geographical and climatic sensitivities, functionality and aesthetics, all of which Boyd felt were hindered by applying European blueprints to Melbourne streets. His 1958-built home – featuring his own range of furniture made with Australian hardwoods and wool fabrics – is now the base of the Robin Boyd Foundation. Check online for upcoming open days to tour this fine example of Australian design.
290 Walsh Street, 3141
+61 (0)3 9820 9838
robinboyd.org.au

Brutalist
Harsh beauty

① Saint Patrick's Cathedral extension, East Melbourne
Worshipful structure

This ecclesiastical gem is both the tallest and largest church in Australia. Designed by architect William Wardell in 1858, and regarded as his most notable commission, the gothic revival underwent restoration work at the turn of the 20th century.

The college building (formerly part of the administration) was replaced more recently by an integrated group of offices and quarters for the resident clergy, the extension of which was overseen by architect Roy Simpson of Yuncken Freeman. His use of a subterranean design around the central circular courtyard, as well as streams running along the roofs, serves to open up the vistas onto the cathedral from Fitzroy Gardens.
1 Cathedral Place, 3002
+61 (0)3 9662 2233
cam.org.au/cathedral

② Total House, CBD
Onwards and upwards

To understand the significance of this TV-like box floating above several storeys of empty parking lots, you have to rewind to the 1960s. It was a time when the motor industry was booming and the city council readily handed out tax rebates for anyone building a car park. Architects were enlisted to create vertical cities whereby the ad men would be able to drive their Ford Falcons and Chrysler Valiants up a ramp, hop in a lift and arrive at the office (swanky bars were, of course, in the basement).

Total House is arguably one of Australia's best examples of such an idea. It was designed by Japanophiles Alan Bogle and Gordon Banfield, who were inspired by modernist great Kenzo Tange, and opened in 1964. In the years since, the oft-misunderstood façade has been faced with demolition many times – indeed, the threat still looms large today, despite the structure securing its heritage status.
Corner of Russell and Little Bourke streets, 3000

3

Plumbers and Gasfitters Employees' Union Building, Carlton
Utilitarian project

The Plumbers and Gasfitters Employees' Union tasked architect Graeme Gunn (*see page 123*) to build its new HQ after it outgrew its last one – informing the choice for a flat roof on his design, should it need to expand further. The resulting polygonal raw concrete structure is one of the state's earliest brutalist pieces.

It was completed in 1970 and became a prominent – and rather alien – structure embedded on the main thoroughfare of Victoria Street. Large industrial, glazed windows interrupt the rough concrete blocks that jut out on the building's front, creating a symbiotic marriage of voids and masses.
52 Victoria Street, 3053

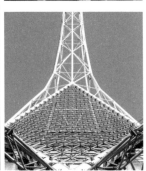

4

Arts Centre Melbourne, Southbank
Heart of the arts

Commissioned in 1960 to give the city a much-needed cultural hub, this complex of ritzy theatres and a concert venue (Hamer Hall) took almost 25 years to complete. Designed by modernist architect Sir Roy Grounds, it was imagined as a subterranean excavation until geographical difficulties demanded the auditorium be raised to almost ground level.

Its iconic spire, which pierces the city's skyline, is no stranger to mishaps either: it was accidentally set ablaze following some frisky New Years Eve fireworks in 2011 and is now safely protected under Victoria's Heritage List. In 2012 the brutalist-inspired Hamer Hall reopened after a AU$135.8m refurbishment led by Melbourne-based ARM Architecture.
100 St Kilda Road, 3004
+61 (0)3 9281 8000
artscentremelbourne.com.au

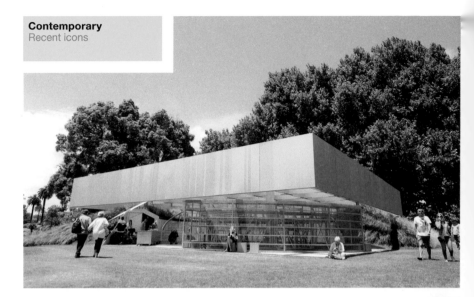

①
MPavilion, various locations
Temporary to permanent

In 2014, Melbourne-based
fashion powerhouse and arts
philanthropist Naomi Milgrom
launched MPavilion, following
a similar format to London's
Serpentine Pavilion. Now
each October to February a
temporary civic space drops
into the Art Precinct's Queen
Victoria Gardens, built to host
more than 300 events during
its four-month tenure.

State and city support and
a healthy budget from the
Naomi Milgrom Foundation
has secured an impressive
roster of architects to design
these venues. Rem Koolhaas
and David Gianotten created
the aluminium grid used in
2017 (*pictured*) while Bijoy Jain
of Studio Mumbai designed
2016's organic hut made from
bamboo, stone and rope, which
is now permanently housed
in the Melbourne Zoo. Other
prior pavilions can be found
at the Hellenic Museum and
Melbourne's Docklands.
mpavilion.org

②

Barak Building, Carlton
Façade with a face

Not only has this 32-storey residential block become a landmark since being unveiled in 2015, it's also become a compelling case study of contentious design. Stand back from the building – the Shrine of Remembrance offers a good vantage point – and you'll be able to see the face of Wurundjeri elder, Aboriginal activist and artist William Barak (1824 to 1903) incorporated into the structure.

There's no denying the talent employed by ARM Architecture to carve out this detailed portrait using the negative space of balconies and the opposing white panels. However, the discord stems from the fact that this act of remembrance for a revered Indigenous elder cloaks the front of 530 luxury apartments, a collision of worlds that's proved too gaudy for some.
551 Swanston Street, 3053

Walk this way
—
Opening up the university buildings on Swanston Street, RMIT University teamed up with Lyons Architecture and three smaller firms to create New Academic Street, an inviting enclave of cafés, laneways, gardens, classrooms and a library.
nas.rmit.edu.au

3

Melbourne School of
Design, Parkville
Education and engagement

Helping to design a building
that sets a global benchmark
for teaching excellence wasn't
enough for Nader Tehrani. He
wanted the Melbourne School
of Design (MSD) to start a
revolution. "I would like to see
things happen in this space we
could never have anticipated
because, in a way, that's the
moment when you know it's
being put to good use," he says.

The AU$129m facility was
co-designed by Tehrani's
Boston firm NADAAA and
Melbourne-based John Wardle
Architects. The contemporary
structure, completed in 2014,
replaced a decaying 1960s
building; a suite of studios
opens onto the central atrium,
which centres on three timber
classrooms that cascade from
the glass ceiling. All adhere to
the two key principles of open
learning and open engagement.
*University of Melbourne,
Masson Road, 3010
msd.unimelb.edu.au*

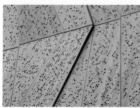

❹ RMIT Design Hub, Carlton
Circular thinking

The Royal Melbourne
Institute of Technology (RMIT)
occupies prime real estate on
centrally located Swanston
Street and this collection of
glass discs sits at the north
end of the university's land
grab. Melbourne architect
(and former professional AFL
player) Sean Godsell designed
the multi-use academic space,
which opened in 2012, to house
architecture, fashion, landscape,
industrial design and gaming
students all under one roof.

Inside, large warehouse-style
spaces are paired with smaller
teaching studios and computer
labs. The underground public
galleries, which are 50 metres
long and nine metres high, host
up to nine shows a year. And
those 17,000 sandblasted glass
discs cloaking the building?
They rotate to both let in and
reflect the sunlight.
*Building 100, Corner of Victoria
and Swanston streets, 3053
+61 (0)3 9925 2260
designhub.rmit.edu.au*

5
Australian Islamic
Centre, Altona North
Modern mosque

This conspicuously modern
building to the city's southwest
is one of the first examples of a
fetching, contemporary mosque
in Australia. The Newport
Islamic Society raised more
than AU$10m and collaborated
with Pritzker Architecture
Prize-winner Glenn Murcutt
and Hakan Elevli for about
a decade to complete the
mosque-cum-community
centre, which opened in 2017.

The sturdy concrete
frame crowned by colourful
triangular skylights moves
away from traditional Islamic
design and opens the space
up to welcome all members
of the public. With a group
that began with just a few
hundred members in the late
1960s growing to be 10,000
strong today, this is a valiant
contribution to the wider
Hobsons Bay community.
Guided tours are held on the
last Sunday of every month.
*23-31 Blenheim Road, 3015
+61 (0)3 9391 0449
australianislamiccentre.org*

Test, test
——
Comprising a network of steel
frames, Testing Grounds is an
innovative example of adapting
place to purpose. Millie Cattlin
and Joseph Norster conceived
the idea of providing temporary
infrastructure to cater for
cultural events and pop-ups.
testing-grounds.com.au

Skyscrapers
Tall storeys

❶
ICI House, East Melbourne
Towering achievement

This glazed slab of an office
block, just beyond the CBD's
border, was what it took to
propel Melbourne's skyline
towards towering corporate
modernism. Opened in 1958,
ICI House (now known as
Orica House) was the city's
first skyscraper and one of the
leading examples to employ
the glass-curtain wall.

Architecture firm Bates
Smart and McCutcheon
(BSM) stepped away from
familiar hard-shell exteriors
and started a new conversation
about the face of urban
buildings. With it came a fresh
approach to construction,
which allowed for the interiors
and external cladding of the
lower levels to be created at the
same time as the steel frames
on the upper levels. ICI House,
with its dusky blue façade,
signifies an important turning
point in Australian urbanism.
1 Nicholson Street, 3002

1 Spring Street, CBD
Bauhaus block

Known for bringing the principles of Bauhaus down under, the late architect Harry Seidler designed this former Shell subsidiary HQ (it's also known as Shell House) in 1985. Located at a southeastern corner of the central Melbourne city grid, the block's curved façade stands on Spring and Flinders streets, maximising views to both the south and east of the city and onto Fitzroy Gardens.

The building's sculptural and opposing curvilinear structure is characteristic of Seidler's work and remains his only completed high-rise project within the state of Victoria. There's a small gallery in the foyer, offering an excuse to check out a limited portion of the building's interiors.
1 Spring Street, 3000

❷
Collins Place, CBD
The Great Space

When IM Pei was awarded the Pritzker Architecture Prize in 1983, the jury cited his ability to create impressive interior spaces as one of his defining qualities. Enter the atrium that lies beneath his two Collins Place towers – designed in collaboration with BSM – and you'll understand what the jury was on about.

This sunken plaza, which is nicknamed the "Great Space", spans six storeys and is a microcosm of city life. The shadow of two soaring finished concrete towers above is softened by the modernist and playful application of a latticed steel-and-glass roof that allows for natural light to illuminate the space.
45 Collins Street, 3000
collinsplace.com.au

Sky high
—

Completed in 1972 with a moody blue, expressed-form façade, the 41-storey 140 William Street in the CBD was designed by Melbourne architectural practice Yuncken Freeman and is one of the city's most beautiful examples of an elegant modernist skyscraper.

4

222 Exhibition Street (Tac House), CBD
A design to reflect on

Sandwiched between Little Bourke and Lonsdale streets, this 30-storey square skyscraper was constructed back in 1988 and served as a forerunner to the city's post-modernist architecture scene. It was designed by Australian practice Denton Corker Marshall, which won the RAIA Merit Award for outstanding commercial architecture upon its completion in 1989.

Its bulky structure is minimised through four reflective glass-curtain walls. These frameless, seemingly floating panels of glass are welded together by a steel grille of balconies that merges at the peak, giving the appearance of four separate blocks.

222 Exhibition Street, 3000
222exhibition.com.au

1

Laneway culture, citywide
Right up your alley

It's an obvious observation –
and definitely one that people
will delight in making when
you say you're planning a
trip to Melbourne – but there
really is something remarkable
about the city's laneway
culture. Melbourne was built
with a European capital in
mind, so its lanes were there
to function as passages to cart
out the waste. It wasn't until the
1990s that trailblazers such as
Meyers Place started opening
bolthole establishments in the
overlooked cobbled corridors.

   Local government wised
up to the potential and
loosened liquor laws, seeing
it as an opportunity to help
combat the CBD's "doughnut
effect". Slowly entrepreneurs
were enticed into the once
empty and staid backstreets
of the business district. The
narrow passageways are now
bursting with kerbside drinking
and dining options, hidden
independent retailers and
ever-changing street art.

2

Skipping Girl, Abbotsford
Sign of the times

Mystery shrouds the identity
of Melbourne's famous red-
dressed darling, who is forever
skipping. Was she a girl who
later became a nun or perhaps
the daughter of a milk-bar
owner? Regardless of her
original muse, Little Audrey
(as she's affectionately known)
was first erected above the
Skipping Girl Vinegar factory
in 1936.

   When the factory was
demolished in the 1960s,

Audrey disappeared – it's
said that Barry Humphries
(also known by the name of his
alter ego, Dame Edna) spotted
her in a car park in 1974 and
laid a wreath for her passing –
but the people of Melbourne
rallied and demanded her
return. The city's activism led
to an updated neon version
appearing along the same
street in 1970.

   Little Audrey is still skipping
(by way of solar power) and
now enjoys heritage status
and maintenance, care of the
Friends of Audrey fund.
651-653 Victoria Street, 3067

❸
Iron lacework, citywide
Signature decoration

There's barely a building
constructed around the turn
of the 20th century that doesn't
wear an iron petticoat. The
obsession was born from the
gold rush boom in the late
1800s: as the city's skyline
shot up and neighbourhoods
sprawled outwards, developers
found themselves with a little
extra cash to splash on design.
Lacework was a relatively
affordable enhancement
and, while the flow of wealth
diminished, the trend for
intricate ironwork long
outlasted the era.

**Architects who shaped
the city**

01 **Robin Boyd:** A key
    influencer of the country's
    modern architecture (*see
    pages 76 and 113*), Boyd
    started a conversation
    about what Australian
    architecture should
    embody, considering its
    look, role and surrounds.
02 **Daryl Jackson:** Jackson
    sees architecture as a
    problem-solving exercise.
    His designs are both
    practical and collaborative
    and his practice has taken
    on large projects such
    as 120 Collins Street and
    the Docklands Stadium.
03 **Peter McIntyre:** McIntyre
    is one of Australia's most
    experimental modernist
    architects. Following on
    from his River Residence
    (*see page 112*), he won
    the bid to design the city's
    Olympic swimming pool
    for the 1956 Games.
04 **Graeme Gunn:** A
    major force in leading
    modernist Melbourne
    through to contemporary
    Melbourne, Gunn won
    the Australian Institute
    of Architects gold medal
    and his work includes the
    Plumbers and Gasfitters
    Employees' Union
    Building (*see page 115*).

Stunning station
———
All sunburnt brick and
glimmering stuccos, Flinders
Street Station opened in 1910.
The Victorian Government has
allocated it AU$100m for a
facelift but it's unclear whether
the Baroque-style ballroom will
be salvaged and reopened to
the public.

Sport and fitness
—— Let's get physical

Melbourne's fitness scene is less in-your-face than, say, its east-coast neighbour, Sydney. That said, there are lots of options when it comes to working up a sweat. The city has leafy parks, riverside tracks and running and cycling paths aplenty. There are also historic indoor and open-water swimming pools, not to mention some impressively designed yoga, gym and climbing spaces.

We've also rounded up the best venues in which to join the Australian Rules fanatics for those of you who fancy just watching. Now all you have to do is make the weighty decision about which colours to sport.

①

Simhanada, Collingwood
Stretch goals

The impressive monochrome space that is Simhanada yoga studio is hitched to the side of a former hotel built back in 1856. Yoga enthusiast or not, it's worth a visit to admire the raw design by Richard Stampton Architects, which combines geometric glass tiles with a twisting steel staircase and a garden of uneven granite boulders.

Studio co-founder Eoin McCarthy wanted the space to reflect the calmness of a Zen monastery and the rugged feel of his native Irish coast. His teachings follow the sequence-led Ashtanga Vinyasa principles. Newcomers are more than welcome but should phone ahead.
62 Easey Street, 3066
+61 (0)3 9417 2825
simhanadayoga.com

One, two, three, heave!

❷

Melbourne City Baths, CBD
Go to great lengths

The Melbourne City
Baths opened in 1860 as an
unpolluted bathing option after
a severe typhoid outbreak was
attributed to swimming in
the Yarra. Now well into their
second century, the fitness
facilities and pool have been
modernised but the historic
exteriors and ornate poolside
balustrades remain.

The centre is a good retreat
in which to swim a few laps of
the 30 metre pool, play a game
of squash, work out in the
gym or join a fitness class. The
setting is also striking enough
that magazines, TV shows
and production companies
regularly use it as a backdrop.
420 Swanston Street, 3000
+61 (0)3 9658 9011
melbourne.vic.gov.au/
community/sports-recreation/
melbourne-city-baths

❸
Northside Boulders, Brunswick
High achievers

From the people who sparked
Melbourne's love affair with
climbing at Abbotsford's The
Lactic Factory comes a bigger
– and, more importantly,
taller – climbing gym. Setting
up in a former artists' shared
space turned illicit drug farm
in Brunswick, Northside
Boulders has created a gym
flooded with natural light,
plenty of greenery (legal, of
course) and walls that tower
up to 4.5 metres and overhang
at agility-testing angles.

All the required kit is
available to hire and climbers
of every ability are well looked-
after. The routes change
regularly and are configured
by different members of the
bouldering community.
329 Victoria Street, 3056
northsideboulders.com

❹
Brighton Baths Health
Club, Brighton
Ocean activities

Another storied swim spot,
Brighton Baths has been
keeping Melburnians fit for
more than a century. Jutting
out into Port Phillip Bay, this
160-metre-long swimming
facility has provided bathers
with a protected salty expanse
since 1881. The enclosure
handily measures 50 metres
across should the lengthier
stretch seem a little daunting.

There's a wooden boardwalk
on which to sunbathe, while
within the complex you'll find
indoor and outdoor gyms
(both with waterfront views)
and a steam room. Classes
include Beach Fit and kayaking
and you can also hire stand-up
paddle boards.
251 Esplanade, 3186
+61 (0)3 9592 7350
brightonbathshealthclub.com.au

Take a hike

There are plenty of opportunities to keep fit while exploring the urban landscape but what about those beachy vistas, ancient forests and iconic fauna so strongly associated with the land down under? Well, you're going to have to venture a little further out of the city for that.

01 **Kokoda Track Memorial Trail:** Named in honour of the Second World War soldiers who fought along the Kokoda Trail in Papua New Guinea, this 3km track is an uphill slog through the Dandenong Ranges National Park. Expect to see tree ferns, manna gums, blackwoods and maybe even the elusive lyrebirds.

02 **George Bass Coastal Walk:** This clifftop walk on the Bass Coast winds for 7km from San Remo to Kilcunda (the Kilcunda General Store is a welcome reward for lunch). It dips up and down over golden sandy beaches but, be warned, the currents are strong (there's a calmer swimming option at Kilcunda). Get up close and personal to banksia trees, black-shouldered kites and nankeen kestrels. In winter, keep an eye out for migrating southern right whales just offshore.

Grooming
Looking good

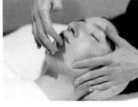

❶
Little Company, Cremorne
Skincare destination

Granted this grooming option is a little further afield, in the eastern suburb of Cremorne, but Little Company delivers the goods when it comes to skincare. New Zealander founder Stacey Burt ties together the simple bedfellows of best products and best care, while assembling just a few trusted brands to work with, including two premium Australian labels, Skin Juice and MV Organics.

Once your nourishing facial is complete, relax a little while longer in the hygge-esque surroundings. Enjoy one of the healthy in-house beverages and be sure to peruse the products on offer before you leave.
79 Stephenson Street, 3121
+61 (0)3 9421 1293
littlecompany.com.au

❷
Human Salon, CBD
Mane attraction

Up the stairs that also lead to Rooftop cinema (*see page 104*) is this mellow space designed by architect Alana Cooke and run by friends Candice Harber and Helen Demos. The hairdressing duo met as apprentices nearly two decades ago but this venture, opened in 2015, is the first time they've styled together. "We do a lot of easy-to-maintain colours and cuts with a focus on keeping the hair healthy," says Harber. "Although being in the industry this long, we can also do a mean blow wave."
3F, 252 Swanston Street, 3000
+61 (0)3 9663 1770
humansalon.com

Spectator sports

01 Melbourne Cricket Ground, Richmond: As its name suggests, this stadium was originally established as a cricket venue. It still hosts state and international matches but for Melburnians, who know it as the "G", it's a nigh-sacred sanctuary of Australian Rules football (see page 81).

02 Docklands Stadium, Docklands: This newish purpose-built stadium, complete with a retractable roof, hosts Australian Rules games, home fixtures of A-League soccer side Melbourne Victory and some minor cricket matches.

03 Flemington Racecourse, Flemington: Though the Caulfield Racecourse is arguably prettier, Flemington has the views of Melbourne's skyline as a backdrop. Much more importantly, on the first Tuesday of November it hosts the Melbourne Cup, known as "the race that stops a nation" – the entire state gets a day off.

04 Rod Laver Arena, CBD: Home of the Australian Open, the first Grand Slam tennis tournament of the calendar year, this place also occasionally hosts basketball, gymnastics and more.

05 Albert Park, Albert Park: This area becomes an international sports venue for one weekend a year (usually at the end of March) when it's converted into the street circuit that hosts the Australian Grand Prix, traditionally the opening meeting of the Formula One season.

❸
Men's Biz, CBD
Golden oldie

The Royal Arcade branch of Nathan Jancauskas' barbershop is tucked away inside Australia's oldest indoor Victorian-era arcade. Pale wood and marble accents adorn the intimate interior, which is occupied by a wall of products and a single barber's chair.

"I wanted retail venues that were small and manageable," says Jancauskas. "We sell products with a lot of history and the arcade reflects that." Inventory highlights include double-edged razors by Dovo, badger or boar-hair brushes by Simpsons and a shaving range from London-based Penhaligon's.
Shop 49, 335 Bourke Street, 3000
+61 (0)3 9442 9308
mensbiz.com.au

Look sharp

One of our favourite men's retailers is also a top stop-off for a clip, cut or shave. In the back of Pickings & Parry (see page 58) you can get a taste of the achingly cool barbers of Melbourne, minus the hoity-toity attitude.
pickingsandparry.com

Runs and cycles
Stay on track

Pound the pavement

Melbourne has a plethora of paths and parks for heading out on a run or exploring on two wheels. Here we've highlighted our top picks to clock some kilometres, whether it be on a city track or off the beaten path in urban bushland. Whichever you choose, keep your eyes peeled for the (friendly) native flora and fauna.

01 Tan Track: So named for its stony colouring, this popular running track is nestled in the verdant pocket that is the Kings Domain and the Royal Botanic Gardens. The well-shaded 3.8km loop takes in a small portion of the Yarra River, runs behind the Sidney Myer Music Bowl, past Queen Victoria Gardens and the Shrine of Remembrance, and along Anderson Street.

02 Merri Creek Trail: Merri Creek starts near Wallan and winds its way through Melbourne's northern suburbs for about 70km before it meets the Yarra River. It's ideal territory for both running and cycling and is best embarked at its southern joining point near Dights Falls.

03 Capital City Trail: This is an almost 29km-long track that runs along the Yarra then loops out to inner eastern and northern neighbourhoods, plus the Docklands. The pretty trail takes in city sights as well as parts of the Merri Creek Trail and the Moonee Ponds Creek Trail. To start, hop on the main Yarra Trail outside Hamer Hall and follow the Capital City Trail signs. It's best tackled by bicycle.

Walks
—— Best foot
forward

Melbourne is made for
walking, whether it's
wiggling your way up and
down the CBD's laneways,
popping into every coffee
shop in North Melbourne
or exploring the leafy
corridors of Abbotsford.
We've mapped out four
routes to help immerse
you in this diverse urban
landscape. And the
good news? Australia's
affinity for awnings will
protect you from the city's
notoriously unpredictable
weather. So get walking.

Abbotsford
Reclaimed land

Abbotsford was once
considered an industrial
wasteland but over the past
two decades it has undergone a
transformation. Small bars and
innovative shops now operate
among the warehouses and
many of the backstreet workers'
cottages have been renovated
into comfortable family homes.

The smell of malt hangs
heavy in the air from the
Carlton & United brewery on
Victoria Street, though it's
increasingly offset by the aroma
of locally roasted coffee. A few
things *have* stayed constant
here: it remains a hub for the
Vietnamese community and
the bushland along the Yarra
River is still pristine. This walk
stretches from "Little Saigon"
in Abbotsford's south to
Victoria Park Railway Station.

Food, farms and favourite shops
Abbotsford walk

Hop off the 109 tram at stop
20 and, adjacent to the Bank of
Melbourne, you'll find **1** *Seoul
Soul*, a Korean restaurant co-
owned by former architect
Insu Kim. Head inside for a
bowl of *bulgogi* (grilled beef)
soup or bibimbap.

Upon leaving, turn left
and continue down the
road for a few minutes. At the
corner of Lithgow Street, pop
into **2** *Little Big Sugar Salt*
for a coffee and something
sweet (the café usually has a
mountain of brownies behind
the counter). Once caffeinated,
continue along Victoria Street
in the same direction.

Stop at the traffic lights
on Walmer Street for a
good view of Abbotsford's
most famous landmark: the
3 *Skipping Girl* sign (or "Little
Audrey", as the locals call her).
Originally erected in 1936, the

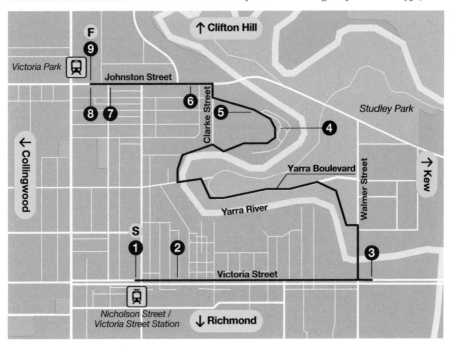

current neon iteration dates back to 1970 (*see page 122*).

Now it's time to go a little bush. Head towards the greenery at the end of Walmer Street and cross the footbridge. Proceed on the sealed path until you emerge at Yarra Boulevard, then turn left and listen for native bell miner birds as you carry on for 500 metres. When the trail forks, set off down the paved route on the left. Cross another bridge, descend the stairs on the left and then follow the river.

You'll know you've arrived at the 4 *Collingwood Children's Farm* when you hear the mooing of cows. Run by a not-for-profit organisation, the project was designed to offer city dwellers a taste of country life and regularly hosts great produce markets.

Give the goats a pat, then climb the trail to the top of the hill and walk through the wooden gates. Continue straight ahead on Saint Heliers Street and you'll soon reach 5 *Abbotsford Convent*, a former convent that now serves as a multi-use arts space with galleries, cafés and artisan studios.

Exit the convent the way you came in and turn left. Carry on until you reach the end of the road, turn right onto Clarke Street and continue until you hit Johnston Street. Turn left here and take a little time browsing the shops along the strip. One that's worth paying particular attention to is 6 *Nicholas & Alistair*, which specialises in rare vintage furniture. Then, a few blocks further up, stop in at 7 *Dutch Vinyl* (*see page 67*). Housed in a former convenience store, this is just the place to sift through a well-chosen mix of records.

By now your stomach is probably starting to rumble, so grab yourself a booth at 8 *Rita's Cafeteria*, located just beyond the rail overpass, and order the linguine with Moreton Bay bug tails (crustaceans). The bar across the road, 9 *Dr Morse*, also serves decent food but the main appeal here is the wide selection of beer from Abbotsford-based craft brewery Moon Dog. Don't fret if you leave feeling a little wobbly; there's a station next door with trains that will whisk you back to the CBD.

Address book

01 **Seoul Soul**
323 Victoria Street, 3067
+61 (0)478 768 760
seoulsoulgroup.com

02 **Little Big Sugar Salt**
385 Victoria Street, 3067
+61 (0)3 9427 8818
lbsscafe.com

03 **Skipping Girl**
651 Victoria Street, 3067

04 **Collingwood
Children's Farm**
18 Saint Heliers Street,
3067
+61 (0)3 9417 5806
farm.org.au

05 **Abbotsford Convent**
1 Saint Heliers Street, 3067
+61 (0)3 9415 3600
abbotsfordconvent.com.au

06 **Nicholas & Alistair**
387 Johnston Street, 3067
+61 (0)3 9486 9595
nicholasandalistair.com

07 **Dutch Vinyl**
269 Johnston Street, 3067
+61 (0)481 882 219
dutchvinyl.com.au

08 **Rita's Cafeteria**
239 Johnston Street, 3067
+61 (0)3 9419 8233
ritasabbotsford.com.au

09 **Dr Morse**
274 Johnston Street, 3067
+61 (0)3 9416 1005
drmorse.com.au

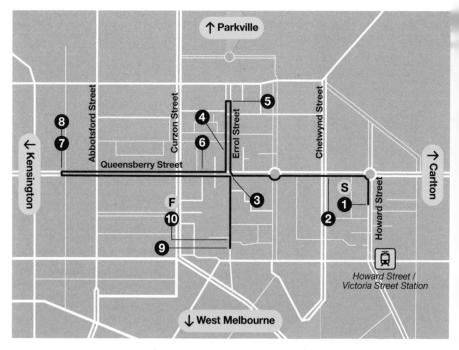

↑ Parkville

← Kensington

→ Carlton

↓ West Melbourne

Abbotsford Street

Curzon Street

Errol Street

Chetwynd Street

Howard Street

Queensberry Street

8
7

5
4
6
3
F
10
9

S
1
2

Howard Street /
Victoria Street Station

North Melbourne
Laid-back hub

This shark fin-shaped neighbourhood can be found – you guessed it – just north of the CBD, wedged between Royal Park and the University of Melbourne to the east and the CityLink arterial road to the west. The suburb was originally a working-class area packed with tanneries and abattoirs – the first development was a cattleyard on what is now the Queen Victoria Market – but today the district is largely residential, with a smattering of independent retailers and smart coffee shops. Much of the action is centred on Errol Street, which has the laid-back feel of a small country town with its wide avenue and awnings with iron lacework.

Bring your appetite
North Melbourne walk

As with most things in Melbourne, this walk starts with coffee. Grab yours to go from **1** *Code Black Coffee* on Howard Street, the North Melbourne outpost of the Brunswick-based roasters.

Flat white in hand, head north to the roundabout then turn left onto Queensberry Street and continue until you

reach **2** *Grigons & Orr Corner Store*, a pint-sized throwback to the milk bars of yesteryear. Resist the comfort-food brunch menu (you'll need your appetite later) and instead pick up a pack of Tim Tams or some other classic Australian confectionery for the road.

Carry on walking west along Queensberry Street and over the roundabout until you reach the intersection with the main drag of Errol Street. On your left you'll find the former North Melbourne Town Hall, which is now home to **3** *Arts House* and its vast programme of events, including contemporary live art and performance pieces.

Turn right down Errol Street and look for the distressed blue façade of **4** *Auction Rooms*, (*see page 24*) set up in the old WB Ellis auction house. You'll be pleased you skipped the food earlier: the brunch menu here is top notch. It's also known for its coffee (courtesy of Small Batch) but if your caffeine levels are in danger of going through the roof, head a little further north on Errol Street to **5** *Mörk Chocolate Brew House.* In a city overrun with coffee shops, this sleek spot offers something a little different in the drinks department. If the day's too warm for hot chocolate, plump for one of their chilled options instead.

Retrace your steps to the crossroads and turn right onto Queensberry Street. On the right you'll find **6** *Martin Fella Vintage*, which is bursting with men's and womenswear items from labels such as Chanel, Celine and Barbour, plus plenty of one-off accessories and shoes.

Carry on down Queensberry Street for a couple of blocks until you reach **7** *Beatrix*. For the sweet-toothed, this will be the icing on the cake. If you only sample one lamington while you're in town, make sure that it's here: baking maestro Nat Paull's rendition is a masterpiece. Think fluffy sponge and homemade strawberry jam, coated in chocolate and topped with toasted shredded coconut.

Once you're done, head next door to **8** *Guild of Objects*. The brainchild of three local potters, this shop stocks ceramics, jewellery and other craft pieces from an impressive stable of Australian makers. Fill your tote with souvenirs before heading back east along Queensberry and taking a right back onto Errol. At the bottom of the street on your right you'll find **9** *Oskar Pizza*, which serves a delicious range of thin-crust pizzas with toppings such as kipfler potato and bull-boar sausage.

After dinner, it's probably time for a cheeky nightcap. Fortunately, the perfect spot is one door down at **10** *Joe Taylor*. Set behind an atmospheric 1900s shopfront, which once housed the appropriately named gentleman's outfitters from which the bar gets its name, this relaxed venue serves sharp cocktails from an extensive list – if you can't find anything you fancy, the staff will, ahem, tailor a drink to suit your mood.

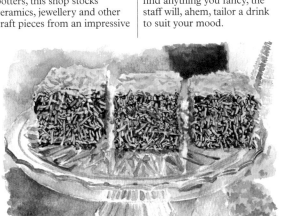

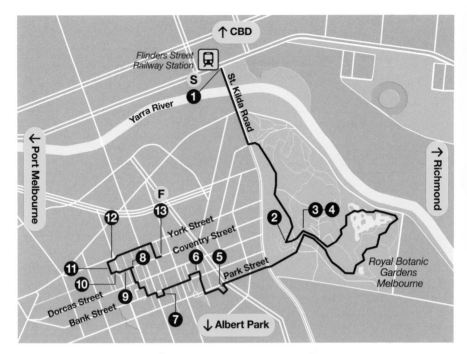

↑ CBD

Flinders Street
Railway Station

S
1

Yarra River

St Kilda Road

← Port Melbourne

→ Richmond

F

12 **13**

York Street

Coventry Street

2 **3** **4**

8 **6** **5**

Park Street

11

10

Dorcas Street **9**

Bank Street

7

↓ Albert Park

Royal Botanic
Gardens
Melbourne

Southbank to South Melbourne
Art beat

South of the Yarra River, St Kilda Road has Southbank's Arts Precinct on one side and 19th-century gardens on the other. The Arts Precinct took shape in the 1970s and the number of galleries, theatres and concert halls has steadily multiplied since.

Crossing to Queen Victoria Gardens, this walk then heads through South Melbourne's mix of industrial and residential buildings. Here shops, cafés and bars pepper the converted terrace houses and factories. South Melbourne Market is one of the area's drawcards, fuelling the area's feel-good vibe since its founding in 1867.

Coffee and culture
Southbank to South Melbourne walk

Exit **1** *Flinders Street Station* on Swanston Street, heading south on St Kilda Road to stroll across the Yarra River towards Southbank's Arts Precinct. Once you're over the bridge take in the cylindrical brutalism of Hamer Hall, followed by the spire of the Arts Centre (*see page 115*), designed by celebrated Australian modernist architect Sir Roy Grounds.

Continue past the National Gallery of Victoria (*see page 96*), where the NGV Design Store is flush with works by Melbourne artisans and makers. Cross the road at the next intersection and enter the gardens to follow the footpath south towards the front elevation of the **2** *Shrine of Remembrance*. Designed by two Melbourne architects (former

soldiers themselves), the memorial boasts a protected sightline looking back towards the city. From this vantage point you can spot buildings by IM Pei, Fender Katsalidis and ARM Architecture ¬ the last of which renovated the shrine in 2014.

Head northeast across "The Tan" (a popular 3.8km running track) and you'll soon arrive at **3** *Jardin Tan*, located next to the 1860s Melbourne Observatory. Pause for a French-Indochinese breakfast at this farm-to-table restaurant owned by acclaimed Australian chef Shannon Bennett then, if the weather is on your side, make a beeline for the nearby **4** *Royal Botanic Gardens*. Walk a loop of this verdant inner-city oasis, exiting by the Macpherson Robertson Fountain and crossing St Kilda Road.

Head straight on Park Street, which will lead you to the

corner of busy Kings Way. Here you'll spot the **5** *City Edge apartments*, a landmark 1970s community-living project that's all brown brick, concrete and wood, and shaded by a canopy of towering spotted gums.

Continue west, then at the Eastern Road park turn right for a filter brew from **6** *Aucuba Coffee*. Turn right as you leave and take the first left to reach leafy Bank Street. Carry on along the road until you spot **7** *Prince Wine Store* and its adjoining bistro, Bellota. Browse the well-stocked wine repository for a bottle by Victoria's The Wine Farm or Mac Forbes, then head next door for a lunch of oysters, charcuterie and cheeses.

Leave via the unofficial back entrance for a quick laneway look-see, where quaint café Wynyard adjoins homeware favourite Made in Japan. Cross commercial Clarendon Street to head west on Bank Street, then turn right on Layfield Street to skirt around the heritage-listed town hall, now home to the National Academy of Music. Continue north past Dorcas Street and into the next laneway. Here you'll discover **8** *Vincent Design*, which stocks a thoughtful medley of "Made in Melbourne" design pieces. A few doors up is textile merchants **9** *Nest*, the shopfront of bedlinen brand

St Marc Linen and also home to products by Sabe Masson, Aesop and Gascoigne & King.

Head across Cecil Street to refuel with an espresso at **10** *Market Lane Coffee*, then cross to the bustling **11** *South Melbourne Market*, where you'll find pastries, cheeses, and chocolates alongside an array of skilfully crafted wares. Reward your walking efforts at **12** *Claypots Evening Star*, where they keep just two beers on tap and the menu features stingray and abalone.

After exploring the market, make your way to York Street and head east. In a few blocks turn right on Yarra Street then left to reach the unassuming terrace house concealing fine diner **13** *Lûmé*. If you're still hungry, you can choose between seven or 14 artful and eccentric courses, such as cauliflower masquerading as camembert.

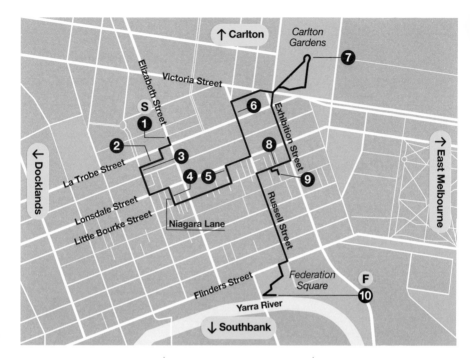

↑ Carlton

Carlton Gardens

7

Elizabeth Street

Victoria Street

S
1

6

Exhibition Street

2

3

8

← Docklands

La Trobe Street

4 **5**

9

→ East Melbourne

Lonsdale Street

Little Bourke Street

Niagara Lane

Russell Street

Flinders Street

Federation Square

F
10

Yarra River

↓ Southbank

CBD
Feel the buzz

A boom in high-rise construction and urban development over the past three decades has transformed the city centre. The major thoroughfares of the CBD are easy to navigate thanks to the Hoddle Grid, the series of streets that sits at an angle to the rest of Melbourne.

But it's when you step off the grid and into the narrow lanes that the city's unique cultural charm comes to life. Popular bars celebrate notorious brothel madams, dark alleys are abuzz with artists and the finest coffee may be sold from a hole in a wall. Like an old W-class tram chugging its way up a hill, Melbourne's journey to cultural capital may have been a long one – but it has certainly arrived.

Bars and backstreets
CBD walk

For more than a century Australia's newspaper of record, **1** *The Argus*, was published in Melbourne until it closed in the 1950s. Start this walk by admiring the plaque on the Elizabeth Street side of the paper's former headquarters at 288 La Trobe Street.

Head west down La Trobe and turn left into the easy-to-miss Sutherland Street. Recall Melbourne's reputation for being a labyrinth of lanes as you turn right into Guildford Lane, a quaint alley that's brimming with shops and cafés. Stop at **2** *Rustica* for breakfast and coffee before continuing to Queen Street.

Turn left and you'll immediately find yourself outside one of the oldest surviving houses in the city centre, **3** *300 Queen Street*, built in 1848 by former mayor

JT Smith. Continue along Queen Street, crossing Little Lonsdale Street, before turning left onto Lonsdale Street and then turning right at Niagara Lane.

Here you'll find a row of petite workshops that are collectively known as Marks' Warehouses. Over generations they have housed everything from bizarre pseudoscience purveyors to popular restaurants. If you're ready

Address book

01 **The Argus**
288 La Trobe Street, 3000

02 **Rustica**
33 Guildford Lane, 3000
+61 (0)3 9642 2203
rusticasourdough.com.au

03 **300 Queen Street**
300 Queen Street, 3000

04 **Sun Moth**
28 Niagara Lane, 3000
+61 (0)3 9602 4554
sunmoth.com.au

05 **Section 8**
27-29 Tattersalls
Lane, 3000
+61 (0)430 291 588
section8.com.au

06 **Russell Street
Police Headquarters**
336-376 Russell
Street, 3000

07 **Royal Exhibition Building**
9 Nicholson Street, 3000
+61 (0)3 9270 5000
*museumsvictoria.com.
au/reb*

08 **Shanghai Village**
112 Little Bourke
Street, 3000
+61 (0)3 9663 1878

09 **The Croft Institute**
21 Croft Alley, 3000
+61 (0)3 9671 4399
thecroftinstitute.com.au

10 **Federation Wharf**
15-19 Princes Walk, 3004

for a tipple, nearby bar **4** *Sun Moth* offers some of the finest regional wines in town.

Exit Niagara Lane and you'll find yourself in bustling Little Bourke Street, with a dizzying array of travel shops. Continue left, passing the old post office and the flagship Myer department store, until you arrive at Tattersalls Lane.

By now you'll have entered Melbourne's Chinatown. Turning left, you'll likely hear the rising sound of revellers enjoying a drink at the ever-popular outdoor bar **5** *Section 8* – why not join them for a swift beer? Thirst quenched, turn right onto Lonsdale Street and then left onto Russell Street. You'll soon arrive at the former **6** *Russell Street Police Headquarters*, the art deco home of the state's police force until the 1990s.

Turn right onto Mackenzie Street and continue to Victoria Street, where you'll soon reach Carlton Gardens, a lush urban space that's also home to the Melbourne Museum and the grand old **7** *Royal Exhibition Building* (*see page 107*), where Australia's first parliament sat in 1901.

Turn left into Exhibition Street, passing Her Majesty's Theatre, and then right into Little Bourke Street. Don't be surprised if you find a queue of hungry diners outside **8** *Shanghai Village* – the dumplings here are famously delicious and cheerfully cheap. Turn left into Paynes Place and then left again into Croft Alley. You may feel as though you've stumbled upon a menacing backstreet but proceed and you'll discover one of the city's hidden rewards. **9** *The Croft Institute* is a bizarre bar with almost as many Bunsen burners as there are cocktails.

Return to Little Bourke Street, continue left and then turn left again onto Russell Street until you reach the intersection of Flinders Street. To your right you'll find the Forum Theatre, one of the city's most popular performance venues. Wander past the theatre, the popular street-art hub Hosier Lane and restaurant staple MoVida Next Door (*see page 40*) to find yourself opposite Federation Square.

Proceed to the farthest corner, where the square meets Princes Bridge, and nip down the set of stairs to discover the collection of riverside bars on **10** *Federation Wharf*. The perfect setting for a late-afternoon drink as rowers glide by on the Yarra and the sun dips below the city's skyline.

Resources
—— Melbourne basics

Your Melbourne to-do list is probably full of flat whites, must-try meals and cutting-edge galleries. But what about hopping on and off those green-and-yellow trams or how to avoid that near-inevitable bout of bad weather? Here we've summarised the best ways in which to dash about town, compiled a list of Aussie slang to whip out at the pub and rounded up which events should be on your radar.

Transport
Getting around town

01 **Flights:** Melbourne Airport, also known as Tullamarine Airport, has one terminal dedicated to international flights and three to domestic flights. Taxis to the city take about 30 minutes and cost roughly AU$60. Alternatively, the SkyBus shuttle drops you at Southern Cross Station and costs about a third of the price of a taxi.

02 **Tram:** Trams will likely be your main mode of transport and they're free within the CBD and Docklands. If heading further afield, be sure to tap on with your Myki card (available at most newsagents and valid on trains, buses and trams).

03 **Train:** Many train lines connect the CBD (from Flinders Street Station) to the outer suburbs and regional Victoria. Again, remember to tap on and off with your Myki card.

04 **Bus:** If a tram won't get you there, a bus will. Use the journey-planner tool on the Public Transport Victoria website. *ptv.vic.gov.au*

05 **Taxi:** Melbourne taxis are plentiful but prices can be steep. As such, ride-sharing apps are popular.

06 **On foot:** It's possible to catch a train into the city centre and explore the retailers within Melbourne Central, Emporium and Myer without stepping foot outside. But please do, because beyond are the layered laneways and neighbourhood strips brimming with retailers and restaurants.

Vocabulary
Local lingo

01 **Pony:** Not a small horse but a small beer, 140ml to be exact

02 **Pot:** Another beer size, somewhere in between a pony and a pint

03 **Dim sim:** Questionable meat dumplings often found in fish-and-chip shops

04 **Parma:** Breaded chicken, covered in passata and mozzarella; a local delicacy

05 **Sook:** Someone who is easily upset or particularly whiny

06 **Rug up:** Dress warmly

07 **Ordinary:** Something bad or sub-optimal

08 **Yahoo:** An uncouth lout

Soundtrack to the city
Top tunes

01 **Weddings Parties Anything, 'Under The Clocks':** An audio tour of 1988 Melbourne by the Aussie folk-rock outfit.

02 **Paul Kelly & The Coloured Girls, 'Leaps & Bounds':** Heavy synths, wailing guitar and melodic lyrics about Melbourne.

03 **Not Drowning, Waving, 'Thomastown':** A yearning track by a group renowned for their depiction of everyday Australian life.

04 **Archie Roach, 'Charcoal Lane':** From the seminal album tackling the harsh modern history of Indigenous Australians.

05 **Courtney Barnett, 'Depreston':** A semi-satirical look at getting on the Melbourne property ladder from one of the country's most revered contemporary voices.

Best events
Just the ticket

01 Australian Open, Rod Laver Arena: The city catches full tennis fever for two weeks in summer. *January, ausopen.com*

02 Saint Jerome's Laneway Festival, Footscray Community Arts Centre and The River's Edge: One of the city's most enjoyed music line-ups. *January/February, melbourne.lanewayfestival.com*

03 Golden Plains, Meredith Supernatural Amphitheatre: Attracts international and local music talent. *March, goldenplains.com.au*

04 Melbourne Food and Wine Festival, various venues: A state-wide celebration with more than 300 events. *March, melbournefoodandwine.com.au*

05 The Finders Keepers market, Royal Exhibition Building: More than 250 independent designers and artists sell their wares. *July and October, thefinderskeepers.com*

06 Melbourne International Film Festival, various venues: One of the oldest film festivals in the world. *August, miff.com.au*

07 AFL Grand Final, Melbourne Cricket Ground: The annual Australian Rules football showdown. *September/October, afl.com.au*

08 Melbourne Cup, Flemington Racecourse: Melburnians take a day off for the biggest horse race in the spring calendar. *November, flemington.com.au*

Sunny days
The great outdoors

01 St Kilda Beach: The 96 tram runs to the beachside enclave of St Kilda and stop 138 is impossible to miss thanks to Mr Moon's wide-open mouth, which serves as the entrance to Luna Park. Take a ride on the Scenic Railway, the world's longest continually operating roller coaster, or continue along the esplanade for St Kilda's popular Acland Street bars and shops. Alternatively, just turn right down Cavell Street towards the city's favourite beach.

02 Melbourne Zoo: When footage emerged in 1963 showing Joy Adamson, author of *Born Free*, sobbing outside the lion enclosure at Melbourne Zoo, it became the catalyst to an ambitious transformation. Throughout the 1970s and 1980s small enclosures were replaced by lush gardens, dusty plains and secluded hiding spots recalling animals' natural habitats. Melbourne now takes great pride in its metropolitan menagerie. *zoo.org.au/melbourne*

03 Alfresco bars: In the early 2000s Rooftop (*see page 104*), doubling as a cinema and bar, opened to instant popularity. Today it seems as if a new outdoor drinking establishment opens its doors almost daily, with the riverside Federation Wharf, Tattersalls Lane and the top end of the CBD among the better areas for sipping under the sun.

Rainy days
Weather-proof activities

01 Undercover retail Alight a metro train at Melbourne Central Station and you're instantly in the heart of the city's main shopping district. The original Melbourne Central was designed by Japanese architect Kisho Kurokawa, a pioneer of the metabolist style. Today's reworked version maintains some of Kurokawa's ideas while being easier to navigate. It leads seamlessly into the Emporium shopping centre while the Myer department store on Bourke Street is reached via an adjoining pedestrian bridge.

02 City Circle tram: Built between 1923 and 1956, the classic chunky design of the W-class tram is a key part of Melbourne's visual identity. It's become an endangered species but its familiar rattle is still a regular presence in the city centre, thanks to the free City Circle route, which allows travellers to take in much of the CBD and Docklands. Trams run in both directions every 12 minutes.

03 Wine tour: The Yarra Valley produces some of Australia's finest wines (*see page 47*) and is less than an hour from Melbourne by road. There are more than 160 wineries producing cool-climate varietals with De Bortoli, Yering Station and Giant Steps among the highlights. Hire a car or book a tour departing from the city centre. Many of the wineries offer luxury accommodation.

About Monocle
—— Step inside

London HQ
Our editorial
office is in
Marylebone

In 2007, Monocle was launched as a monthly magazine briefing on global affairs, business, culture, design and much more. We believed there was a globally minded audience of readers who were hungry for opportunities and experiences beyond their national borders.

Today Monocle is a complete media brand with print, audio and online elements – not to mention our expanding network of shops and cafés. Besides our London HQ we have international bureaux in Toronto, Tokyo, Zürich and Hong Kong, with more on the way. We continue to grow and flourish and at our core is the simple belief that there will always be a place for a print brand that is committed to telling fresh stories and sending photographers on assignments. It's also a case of knowing that our success is all down to the readers, advertisers and collaborators who have supported us along the way.

❶
International reach
Boots on the ground

We have a headquarters in London and call upon firsthand reports from our contributors in more than 35 cities around the world. For this travel guide, two of our resident Aussies – Mikaela Aitken and Ben Rylan – decamped to Melbourne together with Books editor Joe Pickard to explore all that it has to offer. They also called on the assistance of contacts in the city to ensure that we have covered the best in retail, food and drink, hospitality, entertainment and more.

❷
Online
Digital delivery

We have a dynamic website: *monocle.com*. As well as being the place to hear our radio station, Monocle 24, the site presents our films, which are beautifully shot and edited by our in-house team and provide a fresh perspective on our stories. Check out the films celebrating the cities that make up our Travel Guide Series before you explore the rest of the site.

❸
Retail and cafés
Food for thought

Via our shops in Hong Kong, Toronto, Zürich, Tokyo and London we sell products that cater to our readers' tastes and are produced in collaboration with brands we believe in. We also have cafés in Tokyo, Zürich and London. And if you are in the UK capital visit the Kioskafé in Paddington, which combines good coffee and great reads.

4
Print
Committed to the page

MONOCLE is published 10 times a year. We also produce two standalone publications – THE FORECAST, packed with insights into the year ahead, and THE ESCAPIST, our summer travel-minded magazine – and seasonal weekly newspapers. Since 2013 we have also been publishing books, like this one, in partnership with Gestalten. Visit *monocle.com/subscribe*.

5
Radio
Sound approach

Monocle 24 is our round-the-clock radio station that was launched in 2011. It delivers global news and shows covering foreign affairs, urbanism, business, culture, food and drink, design and print media. When you're in Melbourne, tune into *The Globalist* each afternoon to catch up on the world news. You can listen live or download our shows from *monocle.com*, iTunes or SoundCloud.

Priority service — Subscribers save 10 per cent in our online shop

Join the club

01
Subscribe to Monocle
A subscription is a simple way to make sure that you never miss an issue – and you'll enjoy many additional benefits.

02
Be in the know
Our subscribers have exclusive access to the entire Monocle archive, and priority access to selected product collaborations, at *monocle.com*.

03
Stay in the loop
Subscription copies are delivered to your door at no extra cost no matter where you are in the world. We also offer an auto-renewal service to ensure that you never miss an issue.

04
And there's more...
Subscribers benefit from a 10 per cent discount at all Monocle shops, including online, and receive exclusive offers and invitations to events around the world.

Choose your package

Premium one year
12 × issues
+ Porter Sub Club bag

One year
12 × issues
+ Monocle Voyage tote bag

Six months
6 × issues

Chief photographer
Gareth Sobey

Still life
David Sykes

Writers
Sophia Ahmadi
Mikaela Aitken
John Birmingham
Leanne Clancey
Adrian Craddock
Nolan Giles
Myfanwy Jones
Tara Judah
Judith Lucy
Andrew Mueller
Joe Pickard
Linsey Rendell
Ben Rylan
Dan F Stapleton
Jo Stewart
Steve Wide

Photographer
Sean Fennessy

Images
Alamy
Kate Ballis
Tom Blachford
Mark Gambino
John Gollings
Pia Johnson
Trevor Mein
Tatjana Plitt

Illustrators
Satoshi Hashimoto
Ceylan Sahin
Tokuma

Monocle
EDITOR IN CHIEF AND
CHAIRMAN
Tyler Brûlé
EDITOR
Andrew Tuck
CREATIVE DIRECTOR
Richard Spencer Powell

CHAPTER EDITING

M

Need to know
Mikaela Aitken
Ben Rylan

H

Hotels
Mikaela Aitken
Joe Pickard

F ②

Food and drink
Leanne Clancey

R ③

Retail
Joe Pickard

T ④

Things we'd buy
Joe Pickard

E ⑤

Essays
Mikaela Aitken

C ⑥

Culture
Ben Rylan

D ⑦

Design and architecture
Mikaela Aitken

S ⑧

Sport and fitness
Mikaela Aitken

W ⑨

Walks
Mikaela Aitken

M

Resources
Mikaela Aitken
Ben Rylan

**The Monocle Travel Guide
Series: Melbourne**
GUIDE EDITOR
Mikaela Aitken
ASSOCIATE GUIDE EDITORS
Joe Pickard
Ben Rylan
PHOTO EDITOR
Victoria Cagol

**The Monocle Travel Guide
Series**
SERIES EDITOR
Joe Pickard
ASSOCIATE EDITOR
Chloë Ashby
ASSISTANT EDITOR
Mikaela Aitken
WRITER
Melkon Charchoglyan
DESIGNER
Loi Xuan Ly
PHOTO EDITORS
Matthew Beaman
Victoria Cagol
Shin Miura

PRODUCTION
Jacqueline Deacon
Dan Poole
Rachel Kurzfield
Sean McGeady
Sonia Zhuravlyova

Research
Sophia Ahmadi
Melkon Charchoglyan
Dan Einav
Leiah Fournier
Aliz Tennant
Hester Underhill

Special thanks
Emina Adriaans
Christopher Aitken
Louise Banbury
Lucinda Beamish
City of Melbourne
Courtney Holm
Pete Kempshall
Melinda King
Samee Lapham
Erika Nardozzi
Edward Neill
Open House Melbourne
Emma Telfer
Michael Trudgeon
Matt Vines
Visit Victoria

New

The collection
Planning another trip? We have a global suite of guides, with many more set to be released in the coming months. Cities are fun. Let's explore.

Buy today at all good bookshops

You can also visit the online shops at *monocle.com* and *shop.gestalten.com* to get hold of your copies.

Right, where next?